DAUGHTERS
OF
EVE

DAUGHTERS OF EVE

Grace Makau

To order additional copies of this book, contact:
Xlibris
1-888-795-4274
www.Xlibris.com
Orders@Xlibris.com
810387

CONTENTS

ACKNOWLEDGEMENTS

Woman; the inception of what became death; curse was also the vehicle who brought forth Blessing; Life. I'm not being insensitive to modern day enlightened woman but I'm not going to ignore modern day labels placed on the woman either and intend to address the labels as I do the dignified "holy" woman. I thank God for the women in my life who paved the way for the ministry of deliberating and delivering this book. I thank God even for those who challenged me to write about the God in me who makes me a goddess, timelessly (Psalm 82:6; John 10:34). I thank God for the fusion of the deities that abide in me. "Greater is HE that is in me" 1 John 4:4 as it's written. I believe in that "HE-ness, there's She intertwined, just not realized. God created both male and female in His Own Image (Genesis 1:27 although the KJV specifies that "God created he *him*; male and female created He them" signifying (and you're welcome to disagree), HIS fullness was perfected by her so much so that it wasn't good for man to be alone (Genesis 2:18). Perfecting the marriage we experience the "fullness of God" on earth. The Oneness of a male and female intertwined; the left and right brain fusions etc., is His perfection of humankind since "male and female created He them" to be "after His likeness.

I learned through the women who love me to always be true. Being true involves loving, caring and all the virtues that make her, her, in spite of the vices that surround us every day. And the women I refer to bitches, ditches and witches those too, I owe thanks. And I'm not insulting these; more so enlightening those learning how to identify them. Without them, I wouldn't have the power to overcome; without them I wouldn't be who I am today. The law of opposites created a perfection that only the opposite of worlds of women could create. They created both a loving and warrior woman. I love and I fight because of this balance and can't be one without the other.

I learned cold war, I learned how to stand, how to fight the good fight of faith because of the three categories of women. I learned persistence, I learned tenacity and became resilient because of the evil (yes Eve-ill) they constantly hurled and caused me to be on my toes and on watch. I became a watchman because of these. I'll elaborate some more; labels -bitches, (a modern term (label) accepted among certain communities by their own; I'm allowed to use this term (label) because apparently, they use it on themselves as well as on others, in addition to enjoying being called and referred to as this term or label).

My god mother once corrected someone in my hearing when she heard one woman refer to another as a bitch, she retorted how her mother had five children and none of them came out looking like a dog but because of the general acceptance of the ideology until something is done different about it in respect to who we are, bitch is a term that has prevailed in today's vocabulary of description or adverb or pronoun.

Bitches (labels) are the women thought to breed chaos (in more areas than one) with little good to offer; as a result, ensure other else's life is misery. They are characterized as negative; bold in the pursuit of "eve-ill;" their bitch-hood having no shame in their ill-ness, embrace it as who they are. Their lack of acceptance of any others' (positive) truth nor another's way of life and happiness certain; their circumstances (out of no fault of their own), blinds them to the happiness that is due them. Due to lack of exposure to happiness, they cannot or do not realize it, creating a void and need to take learning through a "savior" to illuminate and enlighten them. The "bitch mentality" is often eliminated through positive experiences and because of exposure to the survival mentality, negativity and their lack of knowledge and experience, happiness is deprived. It is written "those who have no knowledge are destroyed." All they know is every man to himself and God for us all. They are openly aggressive and have no couth. And when and if they come out of the low-life stinking thinking, they graduate to the next stage and category.

Ditches (label) are the next step up: They have come to an understanding, educated themselves, understood who they are and they're mission in life. They're not out of the woods yet; but are working on it and so desperately want better so they work towards obtaining a better life. These have somewhat enlightened themselves; they work hard not to return to their former lesser categories and statuses. These still need reformation of a higher kind but their method leaves a lot to be desired. These are known to sabotage others without conscience, warning or remorse on their way up. They survived their old way of life and will not mind taking you or someone else down if it comes to it in order to gain. They have evolved from prey to predator. They're good will towards others is a set up. Their core ill-will when necessary, setting people up, breaking laws as they work towards an accomplishment, that is what ends up happening. These still need to be avoided if possible or as one would put it; play along, play dead, play nice for one's own subsistence. These graduate to the next category.

Witches (label) are the ultimate ill willing women who have mastered the art of being evil undetected. These use psychology, game of words; mind games. They don't necessarily have to be evil themselves but use others (ditches) to carry out eve-ill on others they wish ill upon. They understand deception honestly (being honestly deceitful and deceitfully honest or whichever's convenient). They are in places of authority, or seniority. They understand being amiably nice diverts suspicion from them and often craftily put blame on others in situations they mindfully and carefully perpetrated. You often aren't aware of the origin of the evil if experiencing it because these witches, band together making it difficult to pin point a passive assailant. These aren't even passive aggressive. Bitches often portray aggression. Ditches are passive aggressive. Witches are passive in their methodology with their relations and highly sociable if mingling with them. "Thou shalt not suffer a witch to live" Exodus 22:18, was a widely executed excercise for punishment during the middle ages and centuries prior because of the witches invisible manipulating ability towards innocent peope to satisfy their cravings, propaganda etc. for absolute power and control. It is illegal in certain regions now and murder isn't advised as a medium of change because that too will cost one a life lawfully. Prayer, bible stiudy, meditation, fellowship with the brethren etc. are the various methods to counter withcraft as a remedy; the best solution.

Women, next up from witches are "pre-satanic Eve" and are created to embrace their goodness, Godliness and pass their goodness on from one generation to another. They have embraced the God who created them to be, who God wants them to be, whoever that may be, without threats, or being a threat, without manipulating or conniving their way up or out of anything. These are graceful wisdom women because wisdom only comes from above; from the father of Lights who gives graciously to those who are willing to be who God created them to be.

Blessed of all women is my mother "Rophence Makau," the Queen who loves and cares for me and has shown me that love is unconditional and without love we and I are nothing. Completing my father Bishop Shadrack

Makau; fulfilling HIS image, my mother always taught me to turn the other cheek. I have fallen short in times past at this ideology because like Peter, I have "drawn my sword" of vengeance of judgment and "cut off or plucked off someone's ear" who was otherwise hard of hearing; thrown rocks in suppositions of error. She never runs out of work or propositions, she has always worked as long as I've known her and to fill her shoes I would need to be her, emulated, of which I'm not. My mother has taught and brought to me the unlimited supply of love, grace and faith and why I cannot be defeated by ill-will. Where there's a will, there is a way is a motto I adopted amidst maneuvering ill-will perpetrators. She raised and taught me well and out of those lessons that she has instilled and inspired, I am finding ways to do the same for others. She remains the diamond that inspires value constantly and taught me to utilize my gifts for the good of me and others. She is the Proverbs 31 woman and the woman who inspires wisdom; the perfection of woman only God bestows.

Annie R.E.D. Lee, the jewel that kept me going, hoping against hope, that hope would bring hope; good, in spite of the ill-will perpetrators. She was the soldier that inspired the fighter in me to reappear. As a sitting duck; she assured me; she would always be there and has been since. She was the one jewel that stayed with me when all others couldn't take the cup bestowed upon me. That cup, she partook in. Talk about "happy is to care; happy is to share, one another's burdens, that's why we're here." That is not only a song but a scripture she has lived. She has lived the life; a woman-mother, wife and warrior. The warrior in me was partly shaped and inspired by her. Her struggles and challenges created the balance I describe; the yin and the yang that has created a perfect woman.

PREFACE

Virtues have dissipated and decimated in this great myriad of living leaving a void that needs filling. Women of this age have forgotten where they've come from replacing the values and virtues that brought them their glory with vices destroying the essence of their being. I'm not talking about child bearing or rearing, I'm talking honor, nobility and giving honor to who honor's due, clouding their existence with vain glory omitting what's essential. I feel as a woman, my responsibility by the powers vested in me, is to shed light based on my own experiences eliminating unhealthy competition, as GOD allowed me to see and experience the destructive paths and patterns, "setting aside the things that so easily beset us," pressing on to the greatness they crave allowing personal (emotional) feelings, pride and prejudices which are temporal to be the focus and the center of this journey. "Seeking those things which are above where Christ sits" is no longer regarded in society, caving in to societal pressures women have sold themselves out and sold themselves short, exposed them and others like them to quarry becoming the thing that kept them bound forgetting where and who gave them the power. Well, it usually doesn't take long for powers to be overtaken and overturned as it's written in Daniel, "He changes the times and seasons; He removes kings and sets up kings; He gives wisdom to the wise and knowledge to them who have understanding; He reveals the deep and secret things; _He knows what is in the darkness, and The Light dwells WITH Him_" (Ying Yang) Daniel 2:21-22 in response or reaction to the justices, injustices and health or ills, birthed by the life contributor herself. Did I mention the Deity in charge, though masculine in description has fought for the civil liberties and privileges of the creature he created to perfection; still has the power to destroy the creature that became flawed. We clearly have an adversary since the beginning of time as we known it and it's wise to open the eyes and see as long as GOD gives the capacity and insight and re-evaluate the process and progress much like taking to account all that is, all that has been, reflecting to all that is to come. I'm hoping the Spirit of God will remain your light and your guide as you weave through this journey opened to enlighten and empower. "Women at ease" as Isaiah 32:11-**15**, 32:16-18 it's time for action, the authority was given to make the changes and it's time to harness that Power. The answer is locked in Isaiah 32:11; once this has been accomplished change and restoration will take place. As Mark 5:41 commands, "Talitha Cumi ..I say to you arise" in translation "Damsel -wrapped up in the Word- arise." Even God said "it is not good for man to be alone. Let us make him a help-mate suitable for him" Genesis 2:18. She was born of blessed earth that is man. The one rib short in man was given to her. Proverbs 22:6 "Train up a child in the way that he should go and when she is old, she will not depart from it." One last scripture before diving in, "neglect not the gift that is in thee, which was given thee by prophecy, with the laying on of the hands of the presbytery" 1 Timothy 4:14. The cause and effect, action reaction, stimulus yielding its response chemistry taking place in society as we contrive life is core, precise and hub of our being and consign. Enjoy the reading of this book quenching these vices, being rooted and grounded, walking in love; love being the greatest and not deceiving or being deceived; nor ignorant of the devil's devices, pressing on to the mark of the high calling to which we have been called.

INTRODUCTION

<u>Mitochondrial Eve</u>

The discovery that an ancestral "parent" resided many years ago and originated from Africa was unearthed using DNA. This mother of all is said to have lived some 200,000 years ago. An article was published in 1987 by Cann, Stoneking and Wilson in Nature Magazine brought awareness of the Mitochondrial Eve which ofcourse sparked further interest. This idea had been disputed since the inception of its dispute and the thought that an inherently "black" woman had brought forth all of human life inconceivable. Mitochondrial DNA from cytoplasm organelles discovery that other genetic inherited nuclei cells aside from the 46 cells inherited from both father and mother were found. This ATF energized mitochondrial trace of DNA brought the realization that the DNA cells did not just derive from both parents but singularly from the mother. Regardless of the sperm mitochondrial donation in the process of formation of a human being in the form of fetus, which produces the DNA, it was recently discovered that the mitochondria from its egg even after the fusion of both the sperm with the enzyme breakdown to produce the sperm mitochondria and DNA, it was only the mitochondria from the egg that was used which I understand may be strange, deeming the sperm DNA donation irrelevant beyond conception and only used during the fusion process of fertilization.

With that said, the theory that the XXX chromosomes bearing intelligence from the female egg mitochondria was born, and the transgenerational epigenetic inheritance adopted because of its never changing transfer from one generation to another, from mother to daughter until childbearing ceases, as for the son, the transfer stops at the birth of the son. It is not transferred to the next generation. Only the daughter's gene is carried on with her DNA continued. In essence Adam did not carry on his genetic inheritance, neither did any of his sons. It was his daughters who weren't mentioned in scripture that relayed Eve's inherited DNA which came from Adam and God Himself.

This is where mystery unfolds. The Bible's Eve is said to be about 6,000 years old but her mitochondrial cell DNA is calculated much older. In Genesis 1:1 the earth is said to be created (incepted) along with the heavens but in Genesis 1:2, the earth is said to have been without form (shapeless or unidentifiable), void and darkness reigned upon the face of the deep. This is referred to as the "gap theory." Scientists have been able to prove that Genesis 1:1 was in fact real, that the earth did exists and all its forms and functions but then something happened between vs. 1 and vs. 2 that caused it to become shapeless and unidentifiable, empty and deep darkness covered it.

Mitochondrial Eve was continued in the Biblical Eve; which is why Adam had to be put to sleep to hide the mystery of the centuries old creature brought to him to help him. I began understanding the instinct, sixth sense clairvoyant virtue possessed by women; knowing things by hunch/revelation because they do. They are ancient creatures whos memory though vague has been carried on for centuries and are able to perceive things that aren't quite played out in "normal circumstances." This is the reason why; the mitochondrial DNA lives on and Mother of all carries on.

The only other person who understood this trait or characteristic in Eve was Lucifer who from time after time sought to pollute her inherent DNA and produce his own race. See, the reason why God didn't give angels melanin is because where they are the light emanates from God Himself and do not require the sun to shine on their "earth," The only other person that needed the sun to survive and a way to protect himself from it by converting its radiation into nutrients was Adam and Eve. Lucifer was watching unlike Adam who was asleep. God brought light in Genesis 1:3-5; 1:14-19 and created the lights on the fourth day, which meant that the day He decided to create the man to work the ground needed something extra; melanin for or about the sun. Adam was going to spend a great deal of His time outdoors so there needed to be a way to counter radiation; his coat of many colors provided the safety. Eve had that coat too.

Genesis 6:1-8 narrates a second attempt "non-melanated" people sought to introduce their existence through polluting the mitochondrial make up. Cain was the first of the hybrid from Genesis 3:15 but since there wasn't enough of him, the earth needed more and the sons of God took the daughters of men and reproduced; bringing forth giants. A great mix of human and divine DNA. Eve by herself was divine, a taint of spirit made the gene superhuman.

1

Origin of race/s

We can argue about the origin of race all we want to and not come up with any rational finding as to where races began. Religion, History, Medicine, Physics and Biology all point to one fact; we were all once of one race. Biological researchers have discovered recently all of humanity was grafted out of one woman in Africa; she had to be black. The 3% Far see traits in the blood of every Caucasian and more in other races reflects that the origin of human life was indeed colored. In ancient days albinism wasn't known therefore couldn't be prevented therefore the mass production of "white" babies which created the modern-day Europeans, Asians and other whiter races was orchestrated.

In the Bible we know that up to the time of Nimrod all were one, speaking the same language, of one culture of one mind, from one family until they imagined and began the building of the tower which diverted the worship of one Deity; their Creator to themselves which brought about division of languages. We do not know for sure how far back albinism began but since the time of Adam, scripture has hinted Cain was a biracial child and Abel, pure blooded red man. Also, at the time of Rebecca, the twins of two nations were also considered to be of different races describing one to be "red and hairy" (Esau) and the other "smooth" (Isaac).

Albinism in humans (from the Latin albus, "white"; see extended etymology, also called achromia, achromasia, or achromatosis) is a congenital disorder characterized by the complete or partial absence of pigment in the skin, hair and eyes due to absence or defect of tyrosinase, a copper-containing enzyme involved in the production of melanin. It is the opposite of melanism. Unlike humans, other animals have multiple pigments and for these, albinism is considered to be a hereditary condition characterized by the absence of pigment in the eyes, sditcheskin, hair, scales, feathers or cuticle. Albinism results from inheritance of recessive gene alleles and is known to affect all vertebrates, including humans. While an organism with complete absence of melanin is called an albino (UK /ælˈbiːnoʊ/, or US /ælˈbaɪnoʊ/) an organism with only a diminished amount of melanin is described as leucistic or albinoid.

Albinism is associated with a number of vision defects, such as photophobia, nystagmus and amblyopia. Lack of skin pigmentation makes for more susceptibility to sunburn and skin cancers. In rare cases such as Chédiak–Higashi syndrome, albinism may be associated with deficiencies in the transportation of melanin granules. This also affects essential granules present in immune cells leading to increased susceptibility to infection. This dissention causes loss of pigmentation and transformation of complexion of the skin, hair, eyes etc. making a totally normal colored (pigmented) baby to be born with a different color, changing not only its appearance but race.

Eve was said to have had up to 1500 children sons and daughters alike according to the First book of Adam and Eve. From this family setting came the unknown. GOD in Genesis 2:7 created man "out of the dust of the ground." I don't need to explain what the dirt of the earth looks like to establish my theory that human kind's original appearance was in fact laminated, breathing and living in color. It gets even more fascinating upon exploring further. There's nowhere in the story of creation where blood is mentioned until after the fall which would prove this theory. John 1:4 describes Genesis 2:7. "In him was life; and the life was the light of men." This validated that pre-incarnate Christ "breathed into his nostrils and man became a living soul." Man prefill was a pure form of energy which had no diseases therefore no mucus or blood for him to exist in absolute divinity. Sin brought diseases which triggered the flow of blood and mucus which ultimately brought our demise. Leviticus 11:14 tried to protect the sanctity of the blood from which life flowed by prohibiting the congesting it as does Leviticus 11:17. In fact this law was first given in Genesis 9:4.

My theory suggests when Adam and Eve got kicked out of the Garden of Eden they wound up in the continent of Africa (eventually in their wonderings) having been right located below or within the vicinity of where the Garden of Eden was said to have been located. Additional research into the origin of human race and the division as well is also seen at the Tower of Babel. Nimrod having been the leader of all humanity as they multiplied initiated the building of the tower of Babel. As a result of their shortcomings and pride being a motivator, GOD Himself divinely dispersed this one group of people who only had the one language at the time in all the earth and scattered them sending them away to different lands communicating in different languages; hence the term Babel which means "confusion."

According to this link; (http://science.howstuffworks.com/life/evolution/female-ancestor.htm), which seems much like the first link submitted this report. In 1987, a group of geneticists published a surprising study in the journal Nature. The researchers examined the mitochondrial DNA (mtDNA) taken from 147 people across all of today's major racial groups. These researchers found that the lineage of all people alive today falls on one of two branches in humanity's family tree. One of these branches consists of nothing but African lineage, the other contains all other groups, including some African lineage.

Expounding on the mystery of the branches is reflected in the book of Genesis. The original make-up of the human races was extracted from Adam and Eve. They were and still are our earthly parents. As the family tree grew with all its flaws culminated out of the fall of man, albinism wasn't exempt matter of fact became rampant as the knowledge of science and medicine in limited supply. And then came the flood and by this time races had come to be and become intertwined and integrated with each other which included the race of the giants. I imagine by this time the angels and the human mix had spread to the point where all races had to be annihilated to quench the evil that had grown rampant to the institution and the introduction of the other branches as described in the research containing all other groups.

Even more impressive, the geneticists concluded that every person on Earth right now can trace his or her lineage back to a single common female ancestor who lived around 200,000 years ago. Because one entire branch of human lineage is of African origin and the other contains African lineage as well, the study's authors concluded Africa is the place where this woman lived. The scientists named this common female ancestor Mitochondrial Eve.

The researchers got the idea for this project based on a discovery another geneticist made in 1980. Dr. Wesley Brown noticed that when you compare the mtDNA of two humans, the samples are much more similar than when the mtDNA of two other primates -- for example, two chimpanzees -- is compared. Brown found, in fact, that the mtDNA of two humans has only about half as many differences as the mtDNA of two other primates within the same species [source: Cann]. This suggests that humans share a much more recent common ancestor than other primates do, an idea tantalizing enough to launch the Nature investigation.

The study's lead author, Rebecca Cann, called her colleagues' and her choice to use Eve as the name "a playful misnomer," and pointed out that the study wasn't implying that the Mitochondrial Eve wasn't the first -- or only -- woman on Earth during the time she lived [source: Cann]. Instead, this woman is simply the most recent person to whom all people can trace their genealogy. In other words, there were many women who came before her and many women who came after, but her life is the point from which all modern branches on humanity's family tree grew.

When the researchers in the 1987 study looked at samples taken from 147 different people and fetuses, they found 133 distinct sequences of mtDNA. A few of the people sampled, it turned out, were recently related. After comparing the number of differences among the mtDNA samples within races, they found that Africans have the most diversity (that is, the greatest number of differences) of any single racial group. This would suggest that the mtDNA found in Africans is the oldest: Since it has had the most mutations, a process which takes time, it must be the oldest of lineages around today.

The two distinct branches they discovered contained the mtDNA found in the five main populations on the planet: African, Asian, European, Australian and New Guinean. Researchers found that in the branch that was not exclusively African, racial populations often had more than one lineage. For example, one New Guinean lineage finds its closest relative in a lineage present in Asia, not New Guinea. All of the lineages and both of the two branches, however, can all be traced back to one theorized point: Mitochondrial Eve.

So how did Eve end up being humanity's most recent common ancestor? We'll look at that in this article, as well as some arguments lodged against the Mitochondrial Eve theory. But first, what are mitochondria and why do scientists use mtDNA to track lineage? In a nut shell interracial breeding created multiple races, creating the socio-economic-political and/or religious statuses derived from appearance. As more Albinos were bred, more interracial breeding endured and flourished fulfilling the command God gave to Adam to multiply and replenish the earth.

Christianity, born out of the Judaism was said to have been spread by the white man even though it was started by the Hebrew (Christ). Islam began way after Christians had taken root and flourished amidst persecution from the Romans and their Book written 200 years after its inception. Matter of fact it is known among closed circles that the Council of Nicaea is who weeded out and created the religion. And then there were the worship of other gods and other religions which culminated and emanated from deception from Satan and illusionists of that time. Later on, these groups of people sought to identify and distinguish themselves by looks, creating boundaries, cliques, even beliefs pushing out cultures forming governments. The majority as its known always tended to lead the pack and pushed out minority groups to less desired territories and so the spread of the human race endured. The example of Rebecca's twins is but one example of the birth of mixed races; one Albino, one colored.

Genesis 3:15 reflects the biblical idea of races. It is written "and I will put enmity between thee and the woman, and between *thy seed and her seed*; it shall bruise thy head, and thou shalt bruise his heel." Highlighted the two seeds that had supposedly germinated and the primary reason why God kicked them out of the garden was because of the adulterous relationship (I'm not sure if it happened literally or scientifically) but for sure seed that was germinated inside of Eve's body didn't belong to Adam but Lucifer himself. All through the bible fallen angels were seen to procreate with Adamic women and produced another different race of people that were not purely Adamic.

According to science even bible highlights on the Adamic race as a red (colored race). God having created the sun before man, provided man with a coat of protection against UV rays and the coat I refer to as melanin. Adam's meaning is red man. Ezekiel 28:17 is a small but significant evidentiary description of what Lucifer looked like. It is written "by reason of thy brightness." I believe as Adam was described as a "red man" the brightness in this case was used to describe Lucifer's actual complexion; brightness meaning lightness. Now I'm going to touch on something that is refutable yet proven.

We know that angels were created for work. They are genetically work-o-holics and for this reason, are said to be very productive. But because they were created to serve and work, Adam's work was to rule and reign over the angels who were to work in his domain. Ezekiel 28:16 is a small but significant reflection that he indeed wasn't idle. "By the multitude of thy merchandise" another word for merchandise would be produce, products, goods (business). He was industrious and busy with multiple businesses "full of wisdom, and perfect in beauty."

Thou hast been in Eden the garden of God; every precious stone was thy covering, the sardius, topaz, and the diamond, the beryl, the onyx, and the jasper, the sapphire, the emerald, and the carbuncle, and gold: the workmanship of thy tabrets and of thy pipes was prepared in thee in the day that thou wast created. Thou art the anointed cherub that covereth; and I have set thee so: thou wast upon the holy mountain of God; thou hast walked up and down in the midst of the stones of fire. Thou wast perfect in thy ways from the day that thou wast created, till iniquity was found in thee." Ezekiel 28:13-15.

Genetically, the sardines, diamonds, beryl, jasper etc. stones having been passed down through the genes of the seed of Satan are evidenced in the eyes of most "bright" looking people and a few melanated people. Since we've found in Genesis 3:15 that seed was germinated in Eve's womb which caused Jesus to pronounce judgment on the house that housed the evil seed birthed from sin, by sanctification of the womb by blood on a monthly basis, we know these stones were covered in the eyes of Lucifer which caused his appearance to be most beautiful as described in Ezekiel 28:12 and Ezekiel 28:15 actual translation reads "perfect in beauty."

Cain was what is known today as a demigod (biracial) and Abel was Adamic (red) and from these two races of people (black and white) or should I say bi-racial and black, came the origins of the many races we find today. This racial heritage continued to spawn and spread like fire as people married and were given in marriage and reproduced and replenished the earth. Another example of the angel-man race is seen in the story of Noah.

The book of Enoch was not included in the bible but provided explicit description of Lamech's reaction to Noah's appearance. Book of Enoch chapter 105:1-6 reads that "after a time, my son Methuselah took a wife for his son Lamech. She became pregnant by him, and brought forth a child, _the flesh of which was as white as snow_, and red as a rose; the hair of whose head was white like wool, and long; and whose eyes were beautiful. When he opened them, he illuminated the entire house, like the sun; the whole house abounded with light. And when he was taken from the hand of the midwife, opening also his mouth, he spoke to the Lord of righteousness. Then Lamech his father was afraid of him; and flying away came to his own father Methuselah, and said,

I have begotten a son, unlike to other children. He is not human; but, resembling the offspring of the angels of heaven, is of a different nature from ours, being altogether unlike to us. His eyes are bright as the rays of the sun; his countenance glorious, and he looks not as if he belonged to me, but to the angels. I am afraid, lest something miraculous should take place on earth in his days. And now, my father, let me entreat and request you to go to our progenitor Enoch, and to learn from him the truth; for his residence is with the angels."

Angelic genetic gene was said to be of a "brighter" countenance; unlike the human Adamic race which was said to be darker. Noah's was described as a "white" child born to dark parents to the point where Lamech doubted if Noah was his son because he resembled the angels and not humans.

Returning to the story of creation, we know that the sun was created and melanin was installed for protection against the sun. the way to understand that angelic (white) race of people wasn't designed to live on earth but found themselves here because of the defiance of their ancestors we understand that heaven where the angelic beings lived and worked did not require the melanin "covering" or protection because God Jehovah was their light and His light was not harmful. It's like a litmus test checking for the availability of acidity or alkalinity.

God created man (Adam) to reflect Him. Like looking in the mirror and seeing your reflection in the mirror was and is the concept of creation. Satan made God so angry that He duplicated Himself. Satan's rebellion birthed the creation of many gods so everywhere Satan turned God's image was prevalent to let Him know that He ruled and Reigned on earth and overall and nothing or no-one could replace or dethrone him; a form of punishment for the uprising and the attempt to be like Jesus. God watching Satan like a hawk through his images!

Every white person through DNA is said to have atleast 3% black gene. The whitest of the white has atlease 3% melanin.

2

Covering and the hair

There's a fine line between theology and philosophy; human doctrine and perception versus God's divine order; in an attempt to bring or restore order from what is perceived from a man's perspective to cover up the woman who is or was perceived as vulnerable, weak and needing "intervention."

In the church at Corinth and I believe where this doctrine was inspired, temple prostitutes originally of Greek origin, showed up in shaven heads, (against the Torah where a man's or woman's head should be shaved), in religious gatherings which prompted the discussion of covering, during Paul's time. According to Apostle Paul, he urged women for the sake of the angels to keep their heads covered. Somehow the hair was perceived whether by inspiration or a matter of opinion to be divine and symbol of woman's authority and the longer the woman's hair the greater the glory on her head. It was her divine gift.

Cultural/Ethnic Excerpt:

Throughout the history of woman, hair and texture has always been central. Some textures from some ethnic groups to this day have prompted women to keep their hair short due to the changes which arise from exposure to certain elements such as water i.e. sweat. This "shaving of the hair" was most certainly confused with the temple women characterized by their "uncharacteristic behavior" who shaved their hairs for ease of maintenance." Europe at the time of Christ and earlier was also inhabited by the type of women I'm referring to whose hair textures and maintenance of such included shaving to weave through weather and climactic changes. Adaptation is what I like to refer to. Adapting to the elements enabled women to look at shaving as a form of maintenance for ease and presentability but man thought it not so.

The man however who devoted himself to seek God was set apart as a "Nazarite," like Samson; forbidden to shave his head the entire time of his life, setting him apart for God. Jesus was also deemed a Nazarite set apart for God's work therefore no razor came upon his head. So, hair was most definitely a glorious thing to have but not easy to maintain for others. Locks were invented to ease growth process.

In the story of Samson, no razor was to come upon his head, as were all Nazarite boys sold out as Nazarites and chosen by GOD, mostly first-born sons possessed the same power that was connected to the hair in Nazarites, which was the power I'm referring to here. Shaving it all, meant losing one's power or glory for that matter, therefore the angels who were subject to these female beings, exerted authority over the woman who had her hairs shaven because they didn't see the glory on their heads. I'm not sure if that notion is still carried on today but during that time, hair was crucial especially for women and first-born males.

From this concept of hair being someone's glory brought about the issue of a woman's covering. Women in tabernacle gatherings covered their hairs as a religious notion not as a matter of requirement. It became culture and acceptable form of representation and what was seen or perceived as modest. God did not require man to cover his woman's head. Up until Noah and this too has everything to do with it the introduction of the covering; women walked with their hair as their covering. But the angels in Noah's time were attracted to the beauty of the daughters of the land who were seduced into reproducing with angels and bringing forth angel-man beings which wasn't God ordained but instituted by fallen angels; the Order of fallen angels I might add.

According to Apostle Paul, in 1 Corinthians 11 there have been misinterpretations of his implications. What he implied that referred to a woman's covering during prophesy or in prayer and what ought or ought not to be done. God gave Eve hair when she was created. God, in the presence of His angels, even after they sinned, did not provide the woman Eve an additional covering to cover her covering. God met with them multiple times, and as it's referenced in Genesis, the woman Eve did not appear before GOD with an additional covering on her head and neither did GOD require that she cover up her covering. Quotations from 1 Corinthians 11 is distinctive and contentious among religious groups as the recommendations and requirements of a woman's facial appearance should be.

1 Corinthians 11:1-15 King James Version (KJV)

"Be ye followers of me, even as I also am of Christ. Now I praise you, brethren, that ye remember me in all things, and keep the ordinances, as I delivered them to you. But I would have you know, that the head of every man is Christ; and the head of the woman is the man; and the head of Christ is God. Every man praying or prophesying, having his head covered, dishonors his head. But every woman that prays or prophesies with her head uncovered dishonors her head: for that is even all one as if she were shaven. For if the woman be not covered, let her also be shorn: but if it be a shame for a woman to be shorn or shaven, let her be covered.

For a man indeed ought not to cover his head, forasmuch as he is the image and glory of God: but the woman is the glory of the man. For the man is not of the woman: but the woman of the man. Neither was the man created for the woman; but the woman for the man. For this cause ought the woman to have power on her head because of the angels. Nevertheless, neither is the man without the woman, neither the woman without the man, in the Lord. For as the woman is of the man, even so is the man also by the woman; but all things of God. Judge in you: is it comely that a woman prays unto God uncovered? Doth not even nature itself teach you, that, if a man has long hair, it is a shame unto him? But if a woman has long hair, it is a glory to her: for her hair is given her for a covering."

Now the Nazarite idea was God instituted, even though Paul refuted it. It's very important to set aside what are men's and what's God's. Just like the Pharisees, tricked Jesus with questions about taxes, and Jesus replied that God's money belongs to God and Caesar's, Caesar's. What's God's, is God's and what man's is man's about regarding this.

Breaking it down, during this time the Christian church was facing problems with temple (questionable) women who appeared to services with their heads shaven and Paul so it as a problem because of the original intention of God for the woman as it related to her hair as her covering. Church leaders, mostly comprised of men, were complaining about this new problem in the church and Paul needed to address it. He compared shaving of the head to loss of covering and that women needed to cover their heads because of the angels who saw the woman's hair as the covering of the woman. A woman who had shaved her hair was considered uncovered; the hair was her glory, her power and her protection and the angels recognized her power.

Biologically environmentally, early post Garden of Eden life was brutal and atmospherically exposed to the elements as people lived in caves to keep UV rays from scorching their head and skin and I see why the invention as necessity to "protect" was prevalent. The exposure to the sun while man was required to "till the land" required man to come up with ways to adapt to his environment; making covering of the hair or head necessary because of the elemental factor of UV rays; resulting from environmental factors. We see this invention of additional coverings on the head unfold centuries later, as cultures surrounding the hottest places on the earth (SAHARA etc), also thought to be the region where the Garden of Eden was on the planet.

People around this area both male and female have for centuries maintained their culture of covering of the head even though said to have originated from a religious ideology, it was actually to protect one's head from the beaming and potentially harmful ultra violet rays of the sun. Since the firmament was broken during the flood in Noah's time, the Ozone layer has weakened letting in harmful rays that scorch whatever surface is exposed to it, not just the skin. This factor became religion.

Religions dispute about the origin of Eden, some say it was in actual heaven and the earth location is a replication of the heavenly Eden. But we all agree on one thing, and that's its earthly location. A beautiful fruitful place was turned into a harsh unfruitful hot place. Nothing grows on the Sahara; or surrounding desert regions in the Middle East like the Arabian Desert yet everything grew in the Garden of Eden. It is "mythed" and in fact true that the curse on Cain affected these desert areas which were once fruitful some thousand years after just like death happened to Adam some 900 years later. Cursed was not only the ground for Adam but Cain who shed Abel's blood which was crying out from the ground. Everywhere their feet trod dried up! The tri-fold sin, perpetrated by Lucifer, allowed by Adam embraced by Eve turned a garden into a desert; but that's one theory. Genetically, hair provides a covering; it is made up of dead cells that permeate the scalp from living cells (hair follicles) but is susceptible to harmful rays of the sun and in need of covering in areas where excessive heat is apparent, just as the body needed covering.

Another impression or model of covering was the idea of a husband providing covering to his wife both spiritually and otherwise. A woman was to be escorted out of her father's house (father having been her covering since birth) into her husband's house. This concept dates back to the time of Adam and Eve when God created the woman to be the man's helper. Jesus, in this case, who was depicted as Eve's "dad" (Creator) escorted Eve from his hand to Adam's and from then on Adam, became her covering.

We could look deep into scriptural reference at what transpired at the garden as a result of them separating. As the angels were called to present themselves to God; Adam was left as Eve's covering. The angel that provided spiritual watch over their souls (at this time danger hadn't been discovered to them even though it existed), briefly had to attend to other matters and Adam was to provide that spiritual covering. It is a theory and not speaking as literal doctrine. Some women who aren't "married" have been "covered" by God Himself as we see in scripture God calling His own, His wives; reference Isaiah 54:5 and Jeremiah 3:14.

My spiritual mother, (Annie Lee) remained a widow up until she was 75 years old when she was joined in holy matrimony. Whenever confronted by members of clergy about her "covering," she would retort that her hair on her head was her covering and Jesus was her man. I picked up this ideology to retort to those who confronted me about my relationship status. Jesus understood this as no actual record was found of Him having a woman per say but His followers. It wasn't recorded that He engaged in marital activity, yet He the man remained "married" to His GOD; as GOD. The concept of marriage is a union of spirit, soul and body which is depicted in a marital relationship. This married can be described as fleshly (Adam and Eve reflecting the relationship between God and Man or spiritual (when Jesus comes to reside in our hearts and the Holy Spirit becomes our permanent "roomie" residing inside us, owning and engulfing us with His presence; Who becomes our covering.

Hoping this topic has been exhausted moving on the story of Ruth which is a continuation of the reflection of the covering.

Excerpt:

Apostle Paul, not refuting his doctrine nor the covenant of the Nazarite, I believe was exposed and amidst to this multicultural time as has been since the beginning and was very unfamiliar to the textural context of the hair. On one hand temple prostitution was rampart in that region which could easily confused every other presentation related to hair and put it all in one bundle characterizing appearance and drawing conclusions. There was one very important fact that has been omitted. Culturally, the curly haired woman has had to go unshaven to adapt to climate and weather due to the changes of texture upon exposure of the hair to the elements.

Examining this diagram of hair follicles below, texture is determined by structure of the follicles which in turn produce the various kinds of hair textures. These hair textures adapt different to the elements including but not limited to shrinkage and thickening. It is because of this fact that some women (even men) of a certain culture tend to shave their hair, not religiously or under compulsion to follow a way of life in submission to a thesis or belief system but just simply adapt to the climate and weather.

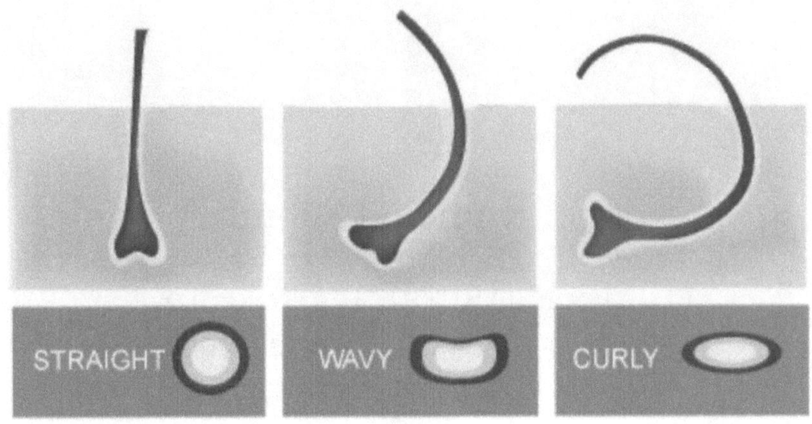

Manageable hair can withstand any type of weather and then there's the type of hair that undergoes extreme catalystic changes depending on what chemical compound it comes in contact with. For example, water can cause hair to be thick and unimaginable when the hair is dried. To combat the thickness due to dryness, many strategies have been invented to maintain a certain texture without it undergoing extreme changes from soft and wav/ straight to brittle, difficult and thick. Water alone can alter the texture of hair in certain cases.

With this insight; looking into this circumstance, women of a certain culture were shaving their hair to combat weather induced adaptations to the texture and appearance in order to manage their hair and showing up at the synagogue and being confused and misunderstood; while mistaken for temple prostitutes. This same group of people genetically are known to be "extroverted" and verbal who tended to have these conversations with Paul while yet he was still speaking which in turn offended the apostle rebuking them to have these conversations and/or questions with their husbands at home to stop the interruptions: References 1 Corinthians 14:34-35.

3

Story of Ruth and Submission

(The book of Ruth): Treating older
women as mothers, younger women
as daughters, peers as sisters

In my opinion the story of Ruth and Boaz are the most fascinating love stories ever; aside from the fact that she came from the most pagan cultures and societies of the time, her mother in law to be had a similar background only more gruesome. Anyone exposed to a life of oppression and slavery of the mind with limited access to freedom and liberties leaves the door open to a better option; is open to a better life and seeks to improve that which seems broken to or in them. Unlike Rahab, Ruth's past didn't involve prostitution or isn't mentioned in detail according to scripture but we know that her culture promoted prostitution through the fertility goddess of their temples in seeking procreating and regeneration through harlot priestesses. So, she was very much exposed to the life of harlotry whether or not she participated.

Acceptance is key in this story. Because Boaz's mother was an outsider, acceptance into "perfection" or what is perceived as perfection is a challenge in itself; Ruth's destiny was ushered in by another. She had a predecessor and what's very important in this story. Her background and origin, and the reason why it would have been impossible for acceptance to take place

14

had there not been a predecessor, helped curve and create the vacuum for acceptance. Unlike the Israelite way of life, the Moab community and life were decked in the worship of many gods in contrast to the monotheistic ideology that molded Israel. The most fierce and gruesome of all was the worship Molech or Moloch. This particular god craved and thirsted for the sacrifice of live babies. In comparison to today's modern culture, the god Molech or Moloch has evolved and what women don't want to accept and blinded by "circumstances," this demon or god still craves for child sacrifices. The method has changed but the outcome is the same. He looks like a goat or is in the form of a goat with two horns poking out of the sides of its head. Much like the one "they" erected in Detroit.

I wouldn't necessarily condemn the choice of refuge Naomi and Elimelech chose as their salvation from famine as God, I believe, turns bad situations into good as long as He's in the misfortune. But this family chose the land of Moab. I could imagine God, in fury, took Naomi's mens' lives away as punishment for choosing to dwell among this particular pagan society being completely aware of their darkness. They could have gone anywhere else but at this time Israel had many enemies as it does today. Mahlon, one of Naomi's sons picked Ruth the Moabitess to wife. Their temples were vile and nothing hallowed. I'd imagine they celebrated Halloween and dedicated their temples to these evil deities who emerge out of evil and none of their intentions were in any shape or form for the good of the people they received worship from.

My opinion about this is based on histories past and God's judgment towards a person according to their dealings and doings as Eve received punishment for allowing an evil seed to permeate and germinate in, her body; and I'm not talking about after the fact, but prevention rather than preservation of evil. In this case Naomi being followed by the curse of Eve playing out in a different circumstance, failed to prevent the vile that clouded and crowded her household by preserving the evil. As man is assigned priest of the home, woman is much the more powerful in propitiating or the provoking the direction of good and evil outcome, through her influence whether or not directly or indirectly she took part in the decision making involving her family. The fact that she was the mother of the home shows that she had the power to direct the outcome because she had the power of influence.

Whether she understood this power that came about by being grafted into Elimelech's life or not, it cost her dearly. God shows no favorites. Her decisions were unpleasant enough to cause the demise of the pillars of her home and household; not one, not two but three. Her three loves were taken from her and she was left without the strength of her life, left to fully rely on God for her strength. My assumption is the men diverted and were wooed into idolatry and pagan way of life knowing very well who they were and What and Who they represented. They were and always would be a chosen generation, a peculiar people, a holy nation. They mixed the holy with unholy profaning themselves as a people by participation and cohabitation. They also could have been intimidated into deviation but that was no excuse with the miracles their GOD was so famous for in delivering HIS own. They were just in the wrong place at the wrong time in history; not Moab.

A little history of how Moab came to be. Moab was the direct result of an "incestral" relationship where Abraham's nephew Lot was lured by his daughters, as he got too drunk to recognize himself, by one of his own daughters; and why God could not accept Moab for one. Another fact is that at the time when Moab was conceived, was during the time when God had just miraculously delivered Lot and his two daughters, from blazing fire and flames of sulfur as it descended upon another pagan world, Sodom and Gomorrah. The only difference in the outcome having seen the past was that God made sure prevention of Moabs and Ammons from happening again and took the men out, leaving the women alive. Men had the bad habit of "losing" control of their minds, and houses, starting with Adam.

Lot wasn't as much a part of Abraham and the Hebraic root. Abraham just didn't want to leave Lot behind as he raised him as his own son. Lot was his nephew. But the Hebraic covenant was with Abraham and his descendants. It was out of mercy that Lot was delivered. Lot came out of paganism and what his daughters performed on him seemed acceptable had they been back home in Ur. Their actions proved their conscience wasn't "processed" as Abraham's was, in spite of the fact that they had been hanging out with Abraham. They knew the God of Abraham by association not by covenant and why they lived. God wasn't obligated to correct them as His own; same thing we see playing out today and why evil persists and good righteous people pay for the evil that's around them. Had there been a covenant with the Hebraic God, either the daughters of Lot or the infants born to Lot by his own daughters would not have survived. They belonged elsewhere; much like the inability or unwillingness to "correct" your neighbor's child when you see them misbehave. You report them hoping their parent/s will do the correcting. God takes care of His own, literally.

So, Naomi loses three men and left with the daughters she gained from paganism *before conception takes place.* Very important to note. God did not allow children to be born to Moloch! Not His own so he made sure he cut off the supply before they actually take root. God intervened divinely by cutting off the supply! I know these seem to be harsh things to say but I have come to understand the mind of God based on observation and personal experiences and that of others. I omit to explain to people who lack the insight and sometimes are learned by experience so I ask God to give them a heart of understanding especially when I know someone's misfortune is directly affecting their outcome. There is always a reason and some reasons are easy to explain to people who don't understand the immeasurable love of Christ. This is one of those examples of God's unfailing love.

Ruth and Orpah may or may not have and based on the circumstances of their location and heritage had ties to the fertility goddess of regeneration through lust with the harlot princess of the temple. It would have been an unholy mix of covenants and pagan seed if conception took place, which would have been raised in an unholy world. God needed Naomi's attention; the men weren't listening anymore, and to get her to return to her home town Israel since God had visited Israel with food and famine ended, He needed to take the misleading leaders of the home, and remove the deception. God never forgets His own and wouldn't want his holy seed mingled with that which is profane. Example? Imagine a combination of Cain and Abel. Even though God instructed through the parable of the seeds and the weeds that they "grow up together," in the end He would separate the weeds from the harvest/fruit in Matthew 13.

There would have been an implosion of the mixed breed; a self-destructive race where Cain would seek to kill Abel; from within himself a conflict would arise and the offspring would struggle to maintain their own sanity without mentioning Ishmael as the epic example and his constant fights within himself between the good and the evil within him. The Abrahamic (good) side of them fights the pagan (Egyptian) side of him affecting sanity which ultimately seeks to destroy the pure good (covenant Israel) (reference: the Middle East). God was preventing insanity by way of eliminating insanity by separation. Abraham lived but his descendants lived to witness or experience the insanity.

Paul described this insanity in detail in Romans 7:21-25 and I quote "I find then a law, that, when I would do good, evil is present with me. For I delight in the law of God after the inward man: But I see another law in my members, warring against the law of my mind, and bringing me into captivity to the law of sin which is in my members. O wretched man that I am! Who shall deliver me from the body of this death? I thank God through Jesus Christ our Lord. So then with the mind, I myself serve the law of God; but with the flesh the law of sin."

They were entertaining evil and God physically had to relocate Naomi and Ruth out of the evil they had entertained back to what God called acceptable. There are things God can't stomach among His own as much as He seems to tolerant. He tolerates Lucifer because he's evil but He won't tolerate Adam for example if He *chose* to be evil. He punished Cain severely but Cain reformed himself through his punishment. Adam reformed himself because of his punishment and his burden. Adam is a piece of Himself, Lucifer isn't and that's the difference. Try and figure him out and realize how complicated a human being he is. His complexity is a signature and a figure of what we cannot fully understand. We are constantly seeking to come to a complete understanding but that will never happen because of Who makes us and What we are. "There is no searching of His understanding" Isaiah 40:28 and for centuries God has been trying to tell Adams who they really are up until Jesus came we couldn't fully understand. Jesus' existence proves the existence and theory of our origin. We look like Jesus because we are a part of Him and are required to live and act accordingly. God had to send Himself to restore himself.

Naomi was the beloved of God and wasn't going to subject her to the madness lurking within her household, her sanctuary and took from her the perpetrators of the evil until they physically left paganism is when God opened Ruth's womb and not until there was a complete baptism into salvation of that time and a complete rejection and denunciation of paganism did she conceive. There had to be a rebirth in Ruth for there to be a birth in and from Ruth and what a blessing she brought forth! The rest is His-story. Orpah rejected her salvation through obedience to her grieving mother in law who she loved dearly (which is why I believe her ending was well) and returned to her pagan infested village. She wasn't fully committed to Israel; her heart wasn't fully "circumcised" but she obeyed. Whether there was reform in her life or not we'll never know. She could have might as well passed the new-found life on to her people but without support I'm not sure how she would have sustained Israel in her and/or her people.

There are two types of examples of submission. Naomi urged Orpah to return to her people because she had no more seed in her to provide for husbands. Orpa didn't realize that she was in covenant with Israel by marriage and what she didn't get about returning to her people meant sticking with Naomi; but she obeyed, and in disobedience to her God, she backslid. There's no doubt that Chilion married a respectable woman in spite of her past in Caanan (Moab) and Molech; which we see later in Rahab. Orpah could have reflected his own mother. She was offered in grief, (and why we shouldn't be making decisions when we're grieving) that she returns to her child sacrificing people whom she had been delivered out from through her marriage to Chilion but because she had nothing more to offer, in spite of the girls' willingness to abide with her and in spite of their losses, Naomi pushed Orpah back into her pagan past. Orpah might still have had a life to return to, but Ruth clearly, did not.

Ruth could have had a more traumatic beginning in the land of her fathers and was determined to disobey Naomi by actually obeying Naomi through insight, unlike Orpah (like Esther did) and earn the lineage of Christ. Ruth caught Naomi on her orders; she understood who her people were and by sticking with Naomi, Ruth understood, Naomi's people were her people and had been her people her entire marriage to Naomi's son. She obeyed the God of her late husband and took Him on completely and followed her mother-in law to her blessing. She somehow perceived her blessing was locked inside, around or through her and wouldn't let her salvation go. Ruth was visionary. She saw the vision and pursued regardless of whether her circumstances revealed her outcome and blessing or not.

The relationship between these three women strikes me mostly because they all got along in spite of their differences. The two girls were Moabitish, and Naomi the stranger. Naturally, I would expect scorn and bias against her for being Jewish but that's not what happened here. Naomi received the respect as mother partly because of the mother-son relationship that would threaten the union of the men they loved had they shown any form of disrespect. Moab was known for its pagan practices leaving the question of values to be desired as it related to social issues and close family ties. We know that there were a lot of child sacrifices whether or not consent was given by family members of the children they sacrificed. One thing is clear, there was a lot of love and respect between the three women, which is reflected and enhanced by their demise.

4

Story of Rahab & Christ's Lineage

(The book Judges): How God respects
THE PRINCIPLE NOT THE PERSON

This is the ultimate love story, one that inspires admiration of Salmon comparing to that of Christ. Salmon I call a hero. He showed his absolute defiance against political religious establishment; against political correctness to love because his wife to be, considered defiled and an outcast according to Jewish law, defied her own people for the sake of Israel, and later Salmon. She hid the spies, risked her own life and those of her family, so that she could blindly secure her own future. It takes blind faith since faith should be blind and activated. What others called foolish had they known, she called faith without ever knowing what faith is. That God does not overlook and handsomely rewards.

A Canaanite woman was a cursed woman. I should bring to your attention what Noah spoke over his grandson because his father uncovered his nakedness. Canaan was scholarly found to be the son of Noah's wife and Ham. There are many questions about the biblical account and what wasn't accounted for. When Noah got drunk, Ham is reported to have slept with his mother? Since Torah's description of uncovering a father's nakedness wasn't the actual unveiling of the private parts to visually set your eyes on one's

20

father's "privacy" but required an action. It could not have been a homosexual act but an actual heterosexual one involving Noah's wife. Now whether Noah's wife was Ham's maternal mother I'm not sure; matter of fact I'm still confused about it. But I know there were 8 people on the ark: Noah and his wife, his three sons and their wives. Ham was still recognized as Noah's son but Canaan may not have been as a result of Ham and his own wife's union but Ham and his mother.

Whatever the background of the story somehow Noah woke up from drunkardness and somehow discovered that one of his sons had (according to the Torah) "uncovered his nakedness." This was an unforgiveable sin; a sin that caused Adam and Eve their paradise which seemed to be following their descendants. Just as the sin of the father was passed down from the father to the son, so do curses unless a Jesus intervenes with obedience. Reflecting on Deuteronomy 28 and Leviticus 26, there are rewards and repercussions of obedience and disobedience. God says when one obeys they are blessed by and because of it; when they disobey they are cursed by and because of it: Cause and effect.

Out of this confusion of family relations was Canaan who was innocent but what he represented wasn't whether he was aware of it or not. But we know God is a God of mercy and is a just God and he lived because there weren't outsiders. Ham should have been the one paying the penalty but Noah for some strange reason and the incestral relations within his family would be the strange reason, cursed his innocent grandson born from his wife, Canaan's mother. That would make a tit bit of sense of why he would attack his innocent grandson. Oh well they were still capsized centuries later because again does not forget. Had they continued in the ways of God they would have survived as a society.

Rahab was Canaanite, her heritage was decked in idol worship and child sacrifices which set Israel apart from them; which made Israel great in the eyes of God and others. The respect for human life wasn't just a conscious realization that people were born to live but that life in itself was precious and life without Life wasn't life and that there wasn't such a thing as death but a passage into another life; an extension of this life that was known to man. And that there were no substitutes to human life and if human beings of the time understood the concept of life would think and do different. But because of the confusion of the gods, mental processes manipulations by genealogies and ideologies of foes kept on the search and pursuit for what they already possessed but could not obtain it until a light bulb was lit in their hearts and minds. They were blind until someone opened their eyes to enable them to see. Their darkness was deepened because of the many generations of sins that were passed down from parents to their children and on and on and on the cycle continued.

A cycle discontinuity was the curse breaker. Rahab according to her capacity continued the lineage of her people, discontinuing the spell against her people, and started her own blessed lineage through Salmon for preserving the life of God's people. Her household was saved which meant that some Canaanite descendants lived on, lived to tell and why the existence of the idolatry in this day and age in spite of Israel's attempt to abolish idol worship.

Hiding of the spies against all odds was heroic at a time when Israel was on conquest, possessing and destroying. Joshua was on a mandate. The children of Israel had made a name for themselves. They were famous for not backing down or out, not retreating or surrendering. They triumphed and were known for it by all its neighbors. Bible records that Jericho their next conquest had heard and they quivered and why the significance of the story. They knew Israel was coming. They were surrounded by an approximately 1.5 to 2 meters high wall (4.9 to 6.6 ft) to 2 meters (6.6 ft) thick and 3.7 to 5.2 meters (12 to 17 ft) high wall, as well as that of the tower suggests a defensive purpose as well. The tower used for ceremonial purposes.

Not only did the 12 spies returned with the fruitfulness of Jericho in the spying escapades prior to the crossing of Jordan to possess it. They; twelve complained about the stature of its inhabitants. They reiterated about how gigantic they were; which raised questions about Rahab's own physical appearance which wasn't emphasized in scripture, having been from the land of giants. Canaan was the land northeast of Egypt, bordered by the Mediterranean Sea on the west, Lebanon to the north, the Euphrates River to the east, and the wilderness of Arabia to the south; to the north was the Hittite Empire and Bashan, to the east were the nations of Ammon and the Amorites, Moab, and Edom and strategically, right smack center of all the nations they were to possess.

Rahab was guilty of treason and was worthy of death. I imagine her profession didn't earn her much respect and how the Israelites or scripture concluded that she was a harlot isn't quite understood; I've searched. Was it because she was kind to the strangers and the strangers mistook her kindness for weakness? I'm not sure but that was the title she earned whether legitimately or not, or could it be her belongings were exquisite enough for men to question her acquisition of them it isn't quite known? Old Testament times (Neolithic ear) of the time had a way to determine whether proven or not whether a woman was questionable to society and Rahab was questionable.

The scarlet ribbon, thread or cloth is one of the "dead" give-away clues that might have suggested that she was indeed a harlot. Either way she endangered herself and that of others. Having known how to manipulate (again here we see a woman's power of influence) Rahab utilized her skill and gift (some would call excellent customer service) and re-directed an investigation of these presumed gigantic search partiers who threatened her life and that of her family too had they in fact caught a glimpse of her dwelling. While the search was on in the direction that she carefully and craftily orchestrated knowing what was at risk, she bought time while the investigated were on her designated path and sent them on their way with a plan; can't beat a woman with a plan. She made sure the pies agreed on her pact; her terms to save her life and that of her families based on what she had done for them. A life for life deal was made. She saved their lives and they were going to save her and her families.

It was a "damned if she did, damned if she didn't" scenario where there was more to lose than there was to gain. But because of the integrity of the spies, Rahab was saved. If for example they were corrupt and didn't honor the "word is bond" treaty they made, Rahab and her family would have been toast. But because of the veracity of the men, Rahab was rescued from her misfortune.

Salmon heard of her brevity and caught his attention. See had there been no principle there would have been no prize. But since God more often than not honors His principle, carved through courage and faith which are all God's principles which Rahab acknowledged without realization of the indoctrination the children of Israel had obtained, He honored His principle. See, spiritual matters all operate on this one principle called faith. Without it the universe and everything formed in and by it would not exist. Rahab being of pagan decent exercised this principle. It is what causes life, and death. Abraham in all his short comings was called a righteous man because of the faith he exercised and the same happened to Rahab.

She went from sinner to saint without actualizing or realizing or even recognizing. Her innocent gesture driven by desperation caused her to be righteous in the eyes of God, so righteous she EARNED the lineage of Christ. Yes, a prostitute became so righteous that she bore the weight of His glory all because of activating the one principle that enables life to endure. She was named in the bible as the ancestor of Christ; she also became the grandmother of Obed, who was Boaz and Ruth's son, who was the father of Jesse who was the legendary general forever honored Prophet, Priest and King David's father, who was Jesus Christ's direct ancestor. Rahab was King David's great, great grandmother. Ruth was King David's great grandmother.

5

Short Excerpt into
The One Eyed Cushite Queen

THE MOST POWERFUL YET IGNORED MONARCH

ONE VERY IMPORTANT FACT:

Without the Roman invasion, there wouldn't be the turn of events that shaped history yet not included in scripture. Christ's birth was said to have been on or around 6BC according to experts. The linage of Joseph or Christ, having had no descendants but we who are Spiritual converts of Christianity are considered descendants of Abraham, would have been history, had it not been for a Cushite one eyed queen who I'm deliberately including in this book, called Queen Candace or otherwise known as Amanirenat (Amanirenas).

History tells us that after the death of Cleopatra, Egypt fell into the hands of Rome through Mark Anthony's successor who wanted nothing to do with her. His predecessors had been married to or lover of the Egyptian queen. Julius Cesar had helped Cleo get rid of all her siblings who upon her father's death was advised to rule with her siblings. She, being the first born thought it unfair, to have to share her rightly earned throne with her younger siblings and sought to kill them all. In the process Egypt formed an alliance with Rome through Julius Cesar. Before long she would appear on Roman coins and Egyptian economy benefited for a while. It was a dangerous bargain which she paid with her own life.

The story of the formidable one-eyed Queen Amanirenat picked up the slack after the reign of Cleo and corrected the mistakes Queen Cleopatra made and fearlessly stopped the unstoppable Roman army from desecrating the African continent by their invasion and conquest and forged a peace treaty, saving the entire African continent. This Cushite Queen Amanirenat, reigned between 40BC and 10BC also enabled Christ to hide in Egypt from Herod who sought to kill him for a good two years. If Rome had conquered the African continent, Egypt and Africa as a whole would have been a part of Roman territory, making it easy to find the Boy-King Jesus Christ who would have been executed as others his age were.

She doesn't get enough praise for the work she did and is deserving of it, regardless of where she originates; i.e. Africa and just like Ruth, Rahab and Bathsheba! She takes the trophy in my books of the most formidable women in history, who shaped history, carved the path Christ took, by saving and/or preserving His life literally, through lineage or otherwise. There are another places Christ could have gone to but God specifically directed Joseph into Egypt! Amen to that!

However, centuries later, since the Europeans of Roman decent who had ruled Europe could not penetrate by force, deceit and trickery (forgetting the peace treaty which the Moors didn't take to consideration, that blood was shed to obtain peace between the two continents). Later the bible was used as the vehicle to "turn the hearts of these men and women" they couldn't conquer, to be subjected to their agenda. The Moors had reigned Europe and N. Africa for centuries and when Spain and Portugal took back their Kingdoms for Christianity, Vasco Da Gamma who may have been enslaved by the Moors sought to look to his former masters to get even perhaps, and send them off to the "newfoundlands" which Christopher Columbus found by the aid of the Moors navigational knowledge of the seas. The Jews and Moors were kicked out of Spain for refusing to convert to Christianity and were thereby given fourteen days to vacate the land. King Charles V and Queen Isabela weren't bargaining on uncertainty and wouldn't waste any time after ceasing back their thrones. The Jews became "nationless" and the Moors returned to Africa. The lost Jews who resided in these West African lands were targeted to work the lands afar off.

Deuteronomy 28:68 confirms the curse which was uttered by Moses during the Exodus from Egypt that if they turned aside from following their true God, these curses would come upon them like a cloak to a body and if they kept their covenant whom their fathers drafted with their God, blessings would come upon them. Having been detached from Israel their land and the rituals that culminated their society and culture, this part of Israel forgot their Lord their God and went after other gods, breaking the covenant between Him and them. This brought on consequences that have been felt for centuries later. God being true to His Word, gave them up. Even though, there were warriors on the African Coast that tried to retrieve the captured African Jews and blood spilled on those beaches, gun powder had not been discovered in the South and was only available to the Europeans and possibly the Moors since they ruled Europe for Centuries.

If you look at Mayan civilizations, architecture etc. today, there are similarities between Egypt and the Native peoples of the "newfoundlands." Deuteronomy 28:68 referred to these lands as" Egypt" not because Egypt's territories spanned so far out, but the migration of ancient "Egypt" (even other African "kingdoms") which had far inhabited these lands since the time of the First Pharaohs. They were known for their Voyages through trade and were known to transport goods to other continents to barter, as seen in Deuteronomy 28:68 (where the rebellious Israel would be taken away in ships). By 3000BC (when the pyramids were known to have first been constructed or began construction) or thereabouts through inspiration of the majestic structures, fixtures or otherwise that preceded them by Nimrod and his Tower and Noah's ark and the giants who inhabited those lands with the Ark floating on water for months until the waters subsided. Noah was alive and about 500 years or so when Abraham was born (according to research); there is said to have been a 400-year gap between them. He lived up to 950 years; 350 years after the flood giving him enough time and population for ship building technology to be passed down and voyages by sea incepted.

In fact, the Africans who weren't even Moors yet at this time were already travelling by sea. Due to cultures and religion interacting with each other which was norm, some of the Arabian (mix of Africa and Asia through interacting and intermarrying) ancestry who at this time were of Moorish "tribe" through religion, began their conquest of Europe by ceasing European ships as they voyaged across the Mediterranean as far back as the 7th Century if I'm not mistaken when Malta was first besieged and became North African territory.

It is safe to say that the descendants of Noah beginning with his three sons had and retained ship building technology which was ultimately passed down to their children and their children after them. Many of them settled in these African regions as well as the Sinai Peninsula in the East and the strait of Gibraltar and Ceuta between Morocco and Spain which separates the Mediterranean and Atlantic in the West and deep into the African continent and mostly around the African coastline because of trade by way of sea which was the most common from of transporting goods to other continents. That's why the ancient empires of the African peoples spanned far and wide. Pirate ships would capture European ships and take captives its people by the time the Moors became Moors.

The pyramids of Egypt are once again seen in the part of the world inhabited by what is referred to as the Mayan or Natives territories thanks to migration by ships built by Noah's descendants who voyaged from the East to the West carrying with them the knowledge of technology required to erect large pyramids and more large ships from the East to the West. Egypt and the neighboring African empires spanned as far West to the Atlantic where the Mediterranean meets the Atlantic and ships were able to pass between the two waters. The Ethiopians and other African kingdoms and empires in the South made the distinction as to where Egypt's and other North African territories ended.

Behaviorally, human sacrifices descended from Cain killing Abel (the first ever human sacrifice) Genesis 4:1-16. So, it is safe and accurate to say that the descendants of Cain through one or more of Noah's children (since intermarrying within families was accepted during that time), migrated to these Western lands and continued their civilizations which originated from Egypt and its pyramids, from Nimrod and the Tower of Babel from Noah himself and his Ark, as the mastermind and Noah got the knowledge from God Himself. In fact, it is very safe to say that the pyramids were inspired by Nimrod and his tower, as the "Titanics" of that age, Noah's ark which settled somewhere on Mt Ararat when the waters subsided.

Studying the environment needed to justify a sacrifice is the condition of the heart (attitude) of the worshipper; and offering sacrifices a form of worship. For example: Cain's state of heart was of worship even though his attitude was indifferent so was Abel's but somehow Abel's sacrifice was accepted and Cain rejected not because of **not** presenting a blood sacrifice as earlier believed and perceived but because Abel brought the *first fruits* of his profession and Cain just gathered whatever he could find for a sacrifice Genesis 4:2-5.

King David is depicted later pouring the water which was brought to him by his "the three mighty men" who broke through the host of the Philistines (Palestine), and drew water out of the well of Bethlehem, which *was* by the gate, drew it and brought *it* to David: but he would not drink thereof, but poured it out unto the LORD" 2 Samuel 23:16. This was accepted by God. It was the state of his heart and attitude that matter which God questioned Cain earlier. God being a principled man could not break His principle of the firsts. These had and still have to be presented today. Learning is what mankind has been doing since the beginning, through trial and error.

Referencing the migration routes and patterns from the time of General Titus and beyond, the Jews (of color), including Jesus always ran to the south and the south camouflaged their existence because of their appearance and have been able to "blend in" with the rest of the population. They blended in so much so that Israel is a subject of geographical dispute; whether or not it belongs to Africa (with it sitting on the African Tectonic plates) or Asia. And then there's Sinai which was inhabited by the Jews some several centuries earlier whom Anwar Sadat took back from Israel. It is believed by most that Israel is in fact an African country. Lebanon isn't far off either. It too sits on the African Tectonic plates but historical accounts on Israel's conquests and habitations suggest that Jews are Africans and not Asians. But who's to argue seeing that Asia has since moved to Africa and Africa to Asia. There's so much "mingling" that telling them apart can be tricky.

6

Heart, and Electromagnetic Power

Learning to be objective

Before digging deeper into the research I would like to point out neurosexism is what differentiates thought patterns, tact, approaches to the object/ subject matter more prevalently than previously thought. It is said of male neuro networks, thought patterns appear more linear which is why men do more compartmentalization and for women their brain networks are more intricately chaotic creating the systematic chaos with thought patterns appearing chaotically organized with the ability to multitask.

"He makes His angels spirits (sons of God) and His ministers a flaming fire (sons of man)" Psalm 104:4.

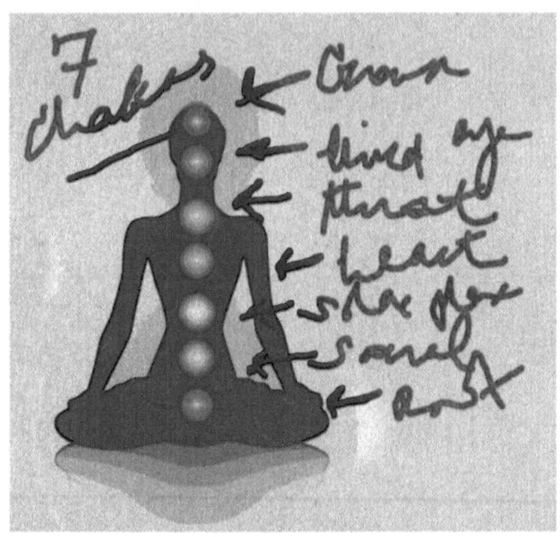

Genesis 9:12-17

[12] "And God said, This is the token of the covenant which I make between me and you and every living creature that is with you, for perpetual generations:

[13] I do set my bow in the cloud, and it shall be for a token of a covenant between me and the earth. [14] And it shall come to pass, when I bring a cloud over the earth, that the bow shall be seen in the cloud: [15] And I will remember my covenant, which is between me and you and every living creature of all flesh; and the waters shall no more become a flood to destroy all flesh. [16] And the bow shall be in the cloud; and I will look upon it, that I may remember the everlasting covenant between God and every living creature of all flesh that is upon the earth. [17] And God said unto Noah, This is the token of the covenant, which I have established between me and all flesh that is upon the earth."

Something the Hindu culture picked up earlier on the rest of us missed is this very very important piece of jistory tied up in quantum. I haven't quite tapped into the correlation between the 7 colors of the rainbow ingraved as the 7 energy centers but I will say, radiation (quantum) has all to do with it. We're surrounded by quantum within without. Below are further illustrations into these facinating energy centers (quantum sources), that radiate within and without.

Noah in Genesis given the rainbow as a sign, token and covenant, judgment by water to that scale wouldn't fal againl. I would therefore like to call it remedy; reminder of God's love by treaty with these radiant colors residing within without. Lets explore further. The order of colors are inverted with the highest color of the rainbow as the lowest color spectrum of the chakra, not signifying anything but rather paying attention the order carries no significant and if it does, I haven't yet discovered the significance. Additional research is found in the passages that follow. We'll retrn to these energy centers and their significance after exploring brain chemistry after the 7 colors of the rainbow below.

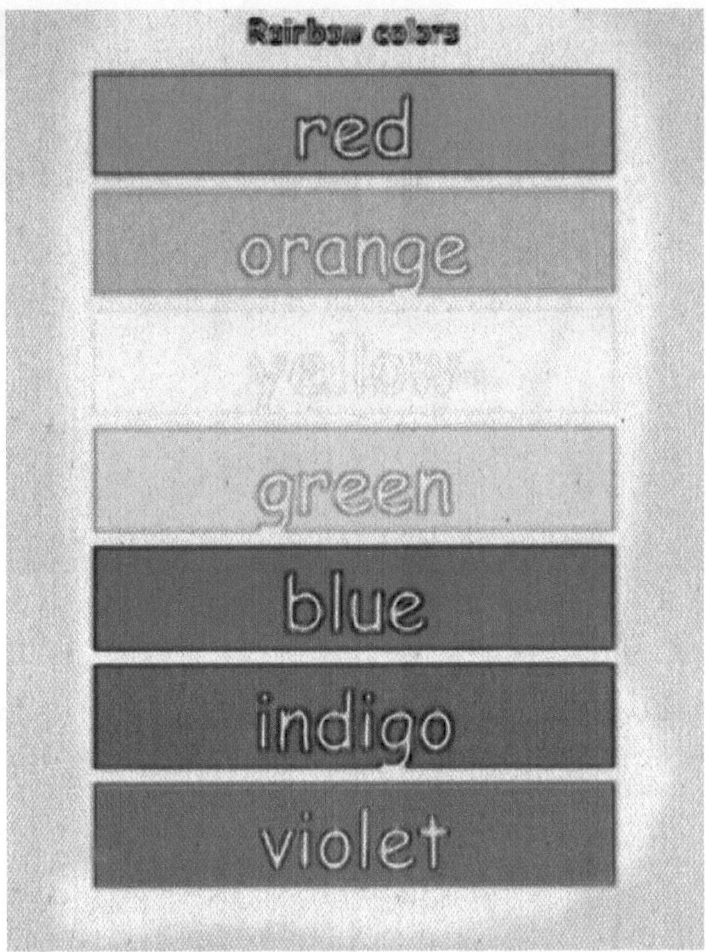

Exploring the notion of pregnancy terminations in this chapter to illustrate its ills and dangers which I'm sure are well known, it is evident that neurological processes and functions begin right at conception. This is known to be true. Nothing is father from the truth that the actual process of conception is very much a neurological process and/or function with hormones and chemicals being released to enable this experience. Throughout the growth process its neurological development doesn't seize. "The **fetal brain** begins to **develop** during the third week of gestation. Neural progenitor cells begin to divide and differentiate into neurons and glia, the two cell types that form the basis of the nervous system. By the ninth week, the **brain** appears as a small, smooth structure."

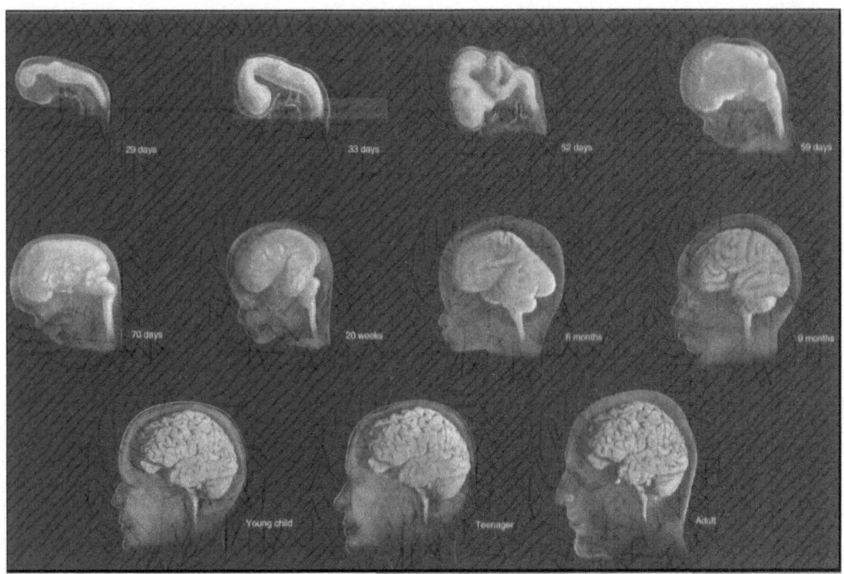

Neurological Consequences:

This is of course enabled and obtained through the processes of fusion and the fusion of processes. The woman could not experience this reality without the man who couldn't separate himself from its conception: All psychology. So it is safe to say that the tampering of this neurological process in fact causes a depletion and deprivation and deficiencies of its hormonal balance required to sustain its development; which is also safe to say that adverse long term neurological effects of tampering with this neurological process causes long term and terminal neurological damage which we refer to as mental illness due to the deprivation of the balance of hormones and neurological process (neurological function) through tampering and termination. This is not explained in its entirety and graphic sense to its "prey." It is withheld instead and society has created a brood of lunatics; the raving kind of lunatics with the government's stamp of approval but that's what medicine is for; to cure dis-eases and medicine is what drives economy.

According to science, and thanks to researchers and books on the subject like "secrets of electricity" by Amin Elsersawi, which provide detailed explanations of the electromagnetic functions, chemically, emotions are tied to chemically emitted components and in the natural latent condition of our bodies, neuron cells are electrically stable and negatively charged. They just hang. The negatively charged neuron cells that collect at the synapse don't have any intensity and are not capable of invoking any emotional impulses, responses, reactions etc. Negativity profits from the potassium inside the neuron cell which contains sodium on the outside. Potassium is more negative than sodium. For example, anger increases the sodium positive ions outside the neuron cell to open the portal where the Sodium on the outside mingles with potassium within. These result in sending positive impulses through the nerves to the heart and brain.

And if you're elated, happy and joyful, a negative impulse will flow in the nerves. The protein of the neuron loves the potassium and hates the sodium, therefore the neuron pumps out the sodium and lets the potassium in, because the sodium atom ends with one electron and the chlorine in the sodium chloride (salt) ends with seven electrons, the sodium atom loses the electron to the chlorine atom. So, the sodium atom becomes a positive ion (cation) and the chlorine atom becomes a negative ion (anion). Balanced electrolytes (the lack of sodium and potassium electrolytes) can reduce critical brain functions. The balance of electrolytes is also important with potassium being needed in larger numbers.

The impulses or urges are sent to the brain, which in turn modulates substances that act as neurotransmitters which can broadly be classified into three major groups: The first would be the amino acids e.g. Glumatic acid, GABA, asaparic acide and glycine etc. The second would be peptides e.g. Vasopression, somatostatin and neurotensions and the third, the monoamines such as neuropinophrene, dopamine, serotonin and acetylcholine.

I'm not in favor of the reputation that clouds women perpetrated by men in very convenient circumstances, derived by conflict. They tend to reiterate and over emphasize the existence of eruptive activity through words or deeds, emanating from the heart fueled by discomfort, displeasure or deprivation of desire. Although true, this truth seems to sculpt its way in "other" people's "observatories" as they examine in scrutiny, micro analyzing its stimulus, cause-effect, and draw conclusions bringing about characterization of an individual; labeling women as "emotional." It's one way to belittle someone at the peak or depths of their moments, implying instability and erratic.

Everyone is emotional, including God; the gravity of the expressions of these emotions are sometimes managed, and are purely biological and genetic to the extent that men are known to be more tactical and rational when angry. Men are known to have better (or should I say) grounding control and effects of their emotional outbursts than women do in certain given circumstances in certain people. Anger in men can come out in extreme aggression, loudness and destructive while in women expressed in escalated words and destructive behavior with words hurling back and forth. However way you look at it, disruptive outbursts occur and can be avoided.

Looking at the physiological compilation of what the easterners would call chakra, or the spinning wheels of energy or energy center in Sanskrit, there are seven energy centers. Each of these centers is associated with specific organs, endocrines, issues, emotions, colors and elements. Balancing these centers can have a physical, emotional and spiritual effect on an individual.

Psychologically, the chemical, electrical, chemical activity of the neurotransmitters transmits or transfer brain cells from the dendrites to the receptors at the synapse vesicle. The synapse creates this electrically charged neurotransmitters as they advanced from chemical neurotransmitters, whereby the chemical particles of the brain cells become electrically charged and get to proceed through the Axum and on to the terminal branches of the Axum; while the negatively charged particles of the brain cells remain stored. What's important about the neurotransmitters is, as they get electrically charged at the synapse, the receptors that receive them have to be compatible to the neurotransmitters or the hormones in order for the transmission to proceed and continue.

Light Encoded Reality Matrix; a scientific term for Aura is comprised of these energy centers that emit energy and reveals in part the energy centers that drives the spectrum of being. With these energy centers, electrical surges (positive emotions producing positive energy) or magnetic pulls (negative emotions producing negative energy and why misery loves company) are felt and/or seen through EKG scale to properly understand sources of pain or joy, making healing apparent by plucking pain or infusing joy and peace.

The Newtonian science is based on the corporal constituents of the cosmos, including humanity and is comprised of matter, DNA; what is factually seen, touched or felt by our physical senses; the components of reality, solid, established and unchangeable. Time here is undeviating, linear.

Quantum science is based on what is not necessarily seen or touched but what is sensed. For example, energy, we know it exists because we feel its effects, gets own deep below the surface and focuses on what's below the stratosphere; surface of the atoms and nuclear, uncovering the energy surrounding it, driving it from within. This is Quantum. I like to give an example of a bicycle. We know what it looks like and what it's for. But in order to realize its full potential one has to make good use of it by actually applying motion; motion generates the energy it needs to fulfill its purpose otherwise it would just appear as an object in its actual form.

Everything is energy, literally and is based on vibrations or movements or motion and frequency (speed/capacity/velocity etc.) and this is what changes or is changeable. Nothing operates without it. Life as we understand it is energy. Suck the life out of us and we remain like the bicycle, in actuality. These vibrations and frequencies are what I or we refer to as the "spiritual components of matter" or the Holonomic Quantum World. This is where it real. There are no limitations. Time is vertical; holographic where time travel (teleportation) is made possible. The ability to make something out of nothing is found here. This is where God our Father lives and beyond. There is no searching of His understanding but the reason why time and space doesn't exist in His world is because He is constantly in this mode and has been trying to get us HIS images to operate in this sphere by faith and believing that life is possible and nothing is impossible.

This is where energy makes something out of nothing. Nothing, doesn't really exist because there's no such thing as nothing. He already exists through energy (production). We are able to connect the breath HE breathed in man in Genesis 2:7 which is also emphasized in John 1:4 to the Breath that is HIM Who is Alive and dwells within us and among us and around us and why meditation is so important therefore encouraged. Scriptural references for meditation that is acceptable for application are as follows:

"Let the words of my mouth, and the meditation of my heart, be acceptable in thy sight, O LORD, my strength, and my redeemer" Psalms 19:14, KJV. "My meditation of him shall be sweet: I will be glad in the LORD" Psalms 104:34, KJV. "O how love I thy law! it is my meditation all the day . . . I have more understanding than all my teachers: for thy testimonies are my meditation" Psalms 119:97, 99, KJV. "This book of the law shall not depart out of thy mouth; but thou shalt meditate therein day and night, that thou mayest observe to do according to all that is written therein: for then thou shalt make thy way prosperous, and then thou shalt have good success" Joshua 1:8, KJV. "But his delight is in the law of the LORD; and in his law doth he meditate day and night" Psalms 1:2, KJV. "When I remember thee upon my bed, and meditate on thee in the night watches" Psalms 63:6, KJV. "I will meditate also of all thy work and talk of thy doings" Psalms 77:12, KJV. "I will meditate in thy precepts, and have respect unto thy ways" Psalms 119:15, KJV. "Princes also did sit and speak against me: but thy servant did meditate in thy statutes" Psalms 119:23, KJV. "My hands also will I lift up unto thy commandments, which I have loved; and I will meditate in thy statutes" Psalms 119:48, KJV. "Let the proud be ashamed; for they dealt perversely with me without a cause: but I will meditate in thy precepts" Psalms 119:78, KJV. "Mine eyes prevent the night watches that I might meditate in thy word" Psalms 119:148, KJV. "I remember the days of old; I meditate on all thy works; I muse on the work of thy hands" Psalms 143:5, KJV. "Meditate upon these things; give thyself wholly to them; that thy profiting may appear to all" 1 Timothy 4:15, KJV.

As you can see, meditation has been encouraged throughout Judeo-Christian existence and is applicable for both spiritual and physical sustenance, rejuvenation, renewal, extension of one's life span, health and wellness to its completion and entirety and people do feel better by taking deep breaths. It is a spiritual healing process as it is a natural one. This very powerful energy field Religion refers to as Spirit is also referred to as the Mysnic Energy Field. This area or the Mysnic Energy Field gets activated (Spirit becomes alive) by the brain in the heart (the enteric brain) or otherwise known as "heart consciousness" producing very powerful mysnic energy fields creating realities by encoding them producing items physically – Human Observership. Do not avenge yourselves but rather give room for wrath is actual and literal. What is in the unconscious is far more than what is in the conscious mind. The BIOMIND has to be at peace. The Manifest Production Observership is based on the conceptual energy reality which is conceptual, interchangeable thoughts producing manifestations and why there is so much power in the tongue.

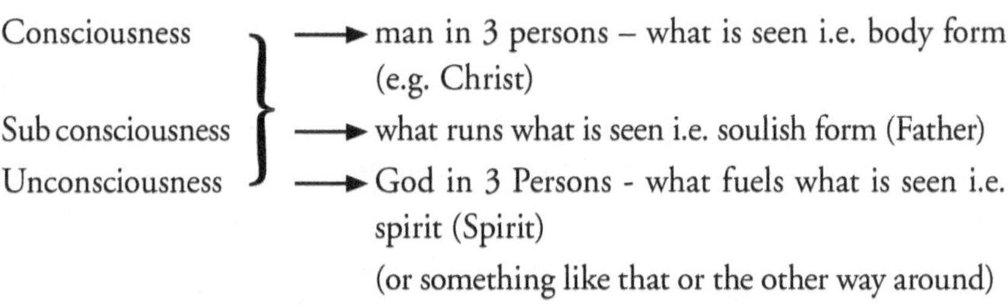

Though patterns, programming or indoctrinations are crucial

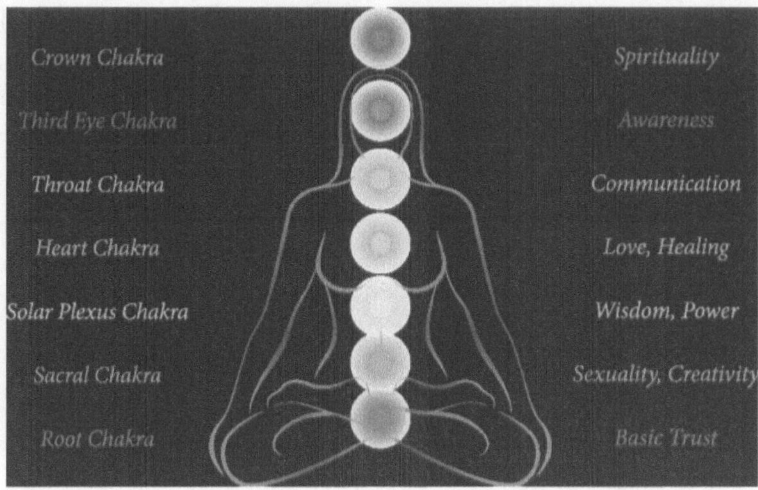

In this figure above, it is not only important that each individual chakra be balanced, but that they also need to be balanced in relationship to each other. Whatever energy is produced here creates your aura. The lower three chakras are considered masculine in nature and call us to action. They help to ground us and are usually concerned with the material world. The higher three chakras are feminine in nature and are associated with self-reflection and the spiritual aspects of life. The heart chakra is balanced in masculine and feminine energy and can help to balance other chakras.

Excessive or moderate brain activity in the primary somatory gland/cortex causes a feeling of rush wind or chill throughout the whole body as though someone invisible is presumed to given a "caressing" touch sensation of the hand whether directly or indirectly throughout the whole body. The healing touch activates or unblocks the flow of electricity in these energy centers that originate from the primary somatory cortex. It is this electrical activity that is activated each time a Reiki session, or a touch session is started beginning with the Crown Chakra, unblocking the flow to generating electricity to the entire body, as the touch session is executed on each energy center, distributing electricity or healing energy to the organs. The crown houses this primary somatory cortex that is activated by touch and in turn sends "shivers down the spine" literally, distributing electrically charged particles throughout the cell bodies and apparently sending healing virtues to the areas or organs that need it. It is both bio-chemical and divine. A fusion and combination of both bio-chemical neurotransmitters and divine energy is needed for complete and balanced holistic health.

The third eye is best explained in Exodus 13.15-16 when the Israelites were in Egypt and needed deliverance. A sealing needed to take place and this sealing through consecration, was directed to the forehead, where eastern mythologists call the third eye. Egyptians adopted this concept which was initiated by the Israelites living in and preparing to leave Egypt. The hands as I explained in the next page, contains the power of healing with the laying on of hands. According to this scripture, the hands were included in the consecration process which enabled blessings to be passed on through them because they underwent the sealing process.

The fusion between bio-chemical electrical chemical process and the divine electrical energy is brought about by the magnetic elements and components within the cells; hence the term electro-magnetic. It is said and found in psychological studies that misery (mostly) loves company. The negatively charged particles and the negative emotions that are distributed around the body create a vacuum and deficiency in the electromagnetic fields in the body creating a stagnation much like stopping water from flowing down stream. Unblocking these fields involves a supply of the positively charged electromagnetic fields to distribute energy throughout these energy centers.

Throat is where words are emitted. Plenty of energy is generated here so much so a person can feel the throat swelling or pressure/tension sensation collecting at the throat depending on the emotion be it anger, jealousy etc. It is in fact "out of the abundance of the heart, the mouth speaks" Matthew 12:34. "Keep your heart with all vigilance, for from it flow the springs of life" Proverbs 4:23. "The good person out of the good treasure of the heart produces good, and the evil person out of evil treasure produces evil;" Luke 6:45.

Heart is above all an organ that has its own brain. Researchers found that there were over 4,000 nerve cells which distinguished it from other organs categorizing it as a thinking organ. It is also associated with Love and Healing; the central epic components that drive the whole structure. Love brings healing, love is healing, and ultimately love is optimum health. One can heal mentally just be receiving and giving love. Love is that powerful. Love is GOD Himself according 1 John 4:7-8. The Revelator urges people in the text to love one another and that if you claim to love God and hate your brother/neighbor then the love of God isn't in you and is named a liar 1 john 4:20. Love dwells in the heart and with and through it expressions of it are processed in the brain and projected via bodily gestures e.g. a hug, a kiss, gently rubbing of the back, other acts of kindness etc.

The gut and gut feeling with its stomach butterflies all falls in the solar plexus sacral energy generating areas. You hear someone has a bad or good feeling about a person or situation or a person has good or bad vibes is as a result of this. Even the Holy Spirit is said to reside in the sacral area which is why and where the "womb" is located. It is the "house" that housed HIM in Mary's story and the house that continues to house HIM even today for those who invite Him in. I use masculine titles when referring to HIM but I have found the Holy Spirit who is also Grace to possessing very feminine characteristics that even Christ and the Father will not forgive anyone who blasphemes Him (Her). Just like a man will not forgive anyone who trespasses a woman he loves, a mother or daughter. The same way a man is possessive and protective over his woman be it mother, daughter, spouse and partner are the same characteristic of how Christ and the Father are towards the Holy Spirit, who is Grace.

The electromagnetic pathways to enable us to connect to a higher power who is the Source and Origin of love is important for normal life. God communicates through these pathways or energy centers. We are able to feel the love of God through these energy centers, which can be interpreted by feelings. He manifests HIMSELF and we feel His Love. His communicates with us and we feel HIS LOVE. Love is one of the fruits of the spirit. Scientifically can be translated as Love is one of the energy centers (I hate the vivid comparison that robs the true meaning of its weight). The Spirit man is said to possess ENERGY or is the Source of the ENERGY we tap into. HE is not justly referred to. HE is a PERSON and not an ELEMENT.

HE IS LIFE SOURCE, the LIFE we live, and THE LIFE HIMSELF as opposed to disparaging description by Japanese Reiki LIFE FORCE. In HIM we live, move and have our being. I absolutely thought to point that out. We cherish HIS Existence, Actuality and Presence as the ENERGY that permeates our bodies and the reason why the heart creates, provides and incubates HIM. The opposite of LOVE is hate. This emotion also contains a source and is influenced by a negative electromagnetic force death. I need not mention the effects of harboring hate would be the opposite of health which would be illness or sickness which in excess would end up causing death.

A hateful heart is a sick heart and as in Proverbs 13:12, "hope deferred makes the heart sick." Proverbs 10:12 "Hatred stirs up strife, but love covers all offenses" 1 John 3:15 "Everyone who hates his brother is a murderer, and you know that no murderer has eternal life abiding in him." Ultimately "whoever says he is in the light and hates his brother is still in darkness" 1 John 2:9. I can go on and on about what the bible says about hatred and its effects which have absolutely nothing to do with wholeness and wellness or health but is associated with sickness, illness, misfortune and death and most of all, the perpetrator of hatred who has nothing to do with health and healing.

"The heart" above all "is deceitful and desperately wicked; who can know it: I the Lord search the heart, I try the reins, even to give every man according to his ways, and according to the fruit of his doings" says the Enforcer. GOD the LIFE GIVE LIFE FORCE LIFE HIMSELF the one we connect with to provide us with the divine energy referred to as SPIRIT searches the heart to ensure we're pure and clean, devoid of ill and maladaptive destructive properties enabling health, wholeness and wellness properties to flow.

Devoid of the electric search creates a vacuum propelled by a craving which ultimately makes the heart sick. That's negative ill flow and because negatively charged neurotransmitters are stored, this vacuum can only be filled by positively charged neurotransmitters that distribute these healing components or particles throughout the whole body.

Every living and non-living object has electromagnetic qualities and capabilities and how we're able to pick up on each other's' feelings and emotions or energy fields. The reason we're susceptible to electrocution is because of this very reason. Electricity is all around us and cannot be denied. It's a fact. Someone makes fun of my psychological escapades and determines that my line of study is actually parapsychological in nature. I reiterate by saying, had there not been the electrical components I wouldn't be able to discern and I hate to say "diagnose" his mental state. As an empath, God has bestowed upon me the gift of determining the various mental problems based on energy and observation as the disturbed seek to describe how they feel. I have had the privilege of accuracy and this particular case stunned his Psychiatrist who diagnosed my friend with an anti-depressant or a hormone because this particular hormone was deficient and in limited supply in his bran.

I wouldn't suggest that one go diagnosing, nay, I have experience and years of research enough not to shy away from it. I don't go around telling people what's wrong with them matter of fact I do the opposite. If I notice an issue, all I can do is sympathize. At times refer people to seek medical help but mostly transfer positive energy to those that need it to the areas that are needed. That is a requirement for a trained master. I read energy fields and from it able to determine where the blockages are. I have been recipient and donor as the body's natural ability to heal itself aids and enables healing to take place.

We're all connected and it is possible to keep out negative depriving qualities that sicken and disable and enforce, emphasize and ensure the positive elements that heal take charge. It's a mind thing; so, we're on to wise mind.

Wise-Mind is the actual pulling together of the reason and emotion creating a rational balance. When one is at reason mind, the heart (emotion mind) doesn't go with it; it's excluded and when one is at emotion mind the reason mind is often excluded. Wise mind incorporates both reason (factual mind) and emotion (impulsive) minds creating a perfect balance in decision making which enables one to NOT be too cruel and heartless or too emotional and irrational.

To avoid irrational, impulsive, not thought out defective of consequential considerations, one needs to operate at wise-mind. It's what cumbers uneven emotional thoughts and cultivates healthy decision making. Above all the scripture encourages, worry about nothing, "be anxious for nothing, but in everything by prayer (or meditation) and supplication with thanksgiving, let your requests be made known to GOD. And the peace of God, which passes all understanding, shall keep your *hearts and *minds in and through Christ Jesus" (LIFE FORCE-according to Reiki, or LIFE GIVER OR LIFE HIMSLEF) Philippians 4:6-& 7.

In Meridians, the Vagus nerve, historically cited as the Pneumogastric nerve, is the tenth cranial nerve, and interfaces with parasympathetic control of the heart, lungs and digestive tract. The Vagus nerves are paired; however, they are normally referred to in the singular. It is the longest nerve of the autonomic nervous system in the human body. As explained in Ameher, meridians consist of twelve pressure points or energy centers that distribute cells to the various organs of the body. The Vagus system unlike the chakra is a little bit more defined and detailed. A healthy Vagus system can revealed a healthy mind or a disturbed ill and traumatized mind with the magnetic poles pulled apart from each other with cells shown to be scattered throughout it. A depolarized mind causes the cells to appear aligned systematically and in sequence with each other throughout the Vagus system. A healthy Vagus system reflects a healthy mind.

It's a fact, meditation (prayer), supplication and a grateful heart are southing properties and powers that promote, permeate peace because it comes from above. A troubled heart is an impulsive, irrational heart. A peaceful heart is an understanding heart.

Meridians contain 12 as opposed or in addition to the 7 energy centers in Chakras which transport energy to the organs that facilitate health. These 12 centers are linked to the central vessel called the Vagus system which channels cells to these centers. Besides giving some output to various organs, the Vagus nerve comprises between 80% and 90% of afferent nerves mostly conveying sensory information about the state of the body's organs to the central nervous system.

The images below are compilation and combination of meridian, Vagus system, another illustration of meridian and another Vagus system respectively.

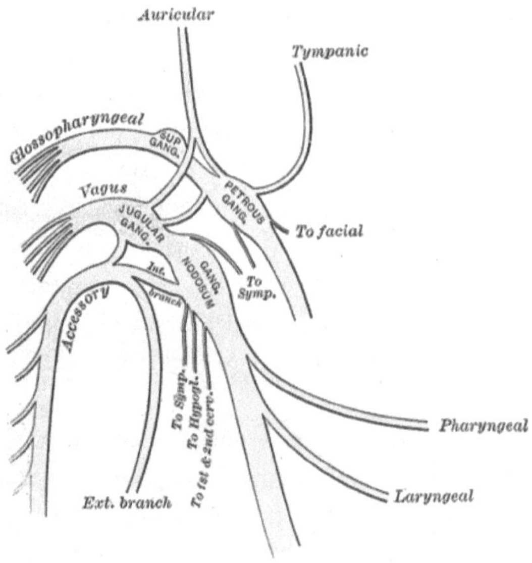

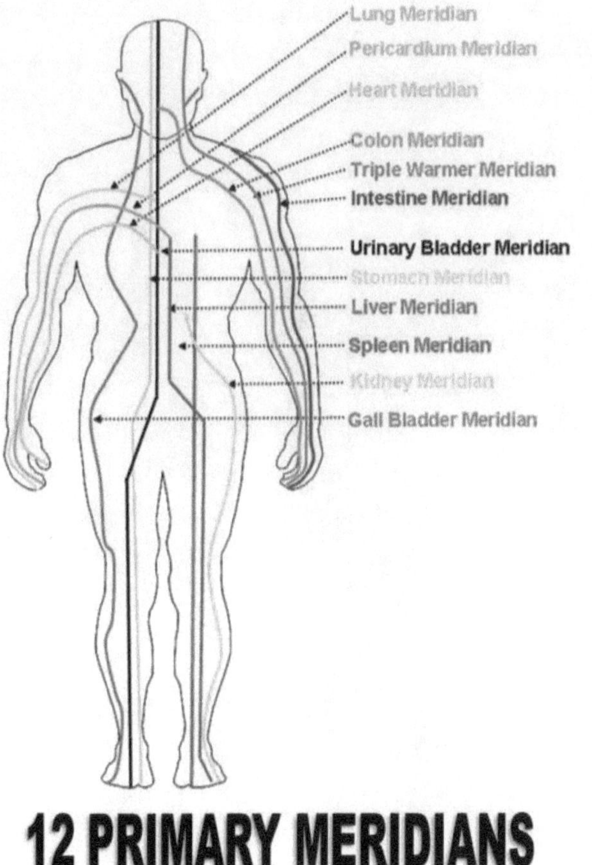

12 PRIMARY MERIDIANS

Like the 12 sons of Jacob or the 12 sons of Ishmael all descendants of Abraham

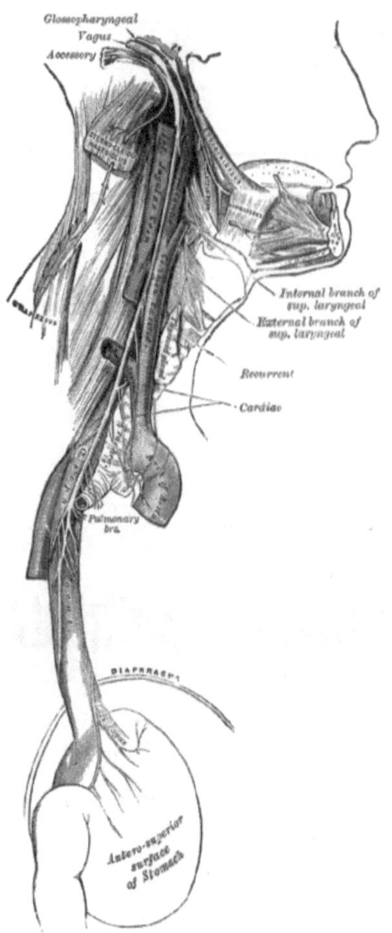

Glossopharyngeal
Vagus
Accessory
Internal branch of
sup. laryngeal
External branch of
sup. laryngeal
Recurrent
Cardiac
Pulmonary
bra.
DIAPHRAGM
Antero-superior
surface
of Stomach

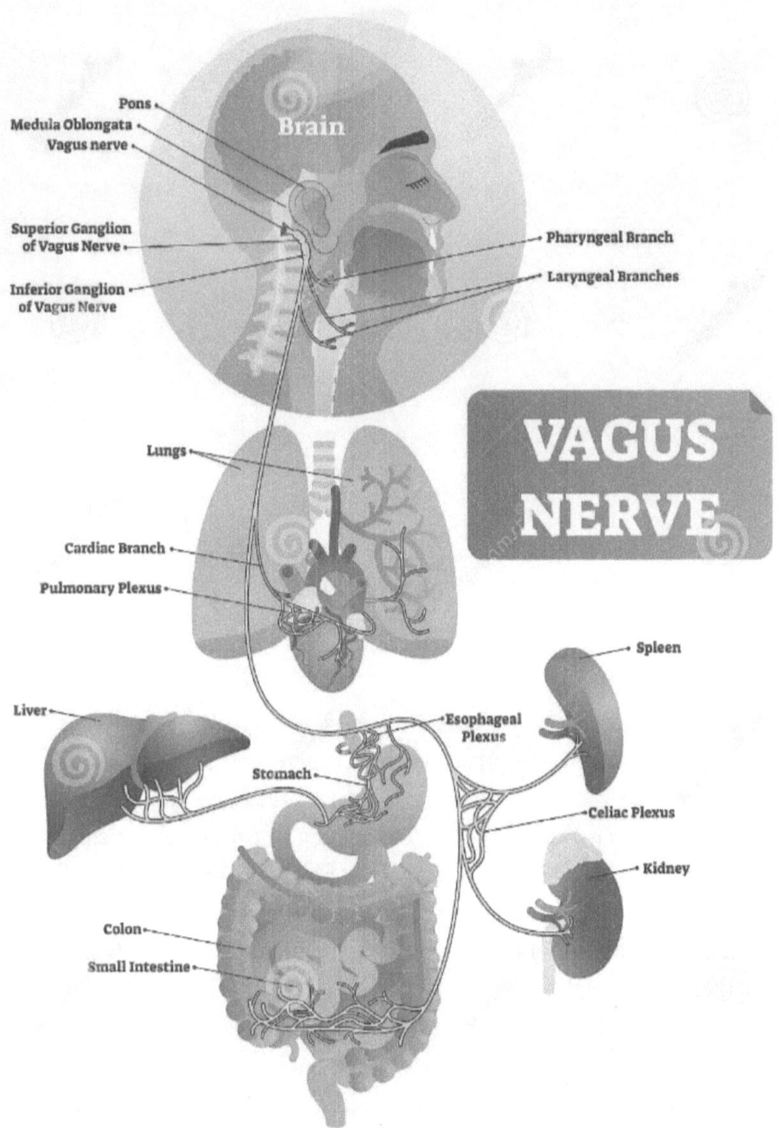

The Vagus System

In practicing meditation and/or prayer or tapping into the Higher Self ensures that energy is evenly distributed to all these vital areas.

7

Undying Love

THE GLUE THAT HOLDS IT DOWN

Genesis 2:7 describes the origin of man; his creation and inception of his life. It is written that after God breathed into his nostrils, man became a living soul and not after blood began to flow. This "breathing" was symbolized by everything I've been exploring. Man was a bag of unseen electrical chemical electrical magnetism which kept him alive. Fluids weren't mentioned because in the medical world fluids are associated with disease. The mucus is disease stricken and the blood where life is said to reside because of sin, disease also dwells therein in.

After the fall of man, it became apparent that blood needed to be shed to atone for the sin. "According to the Law, in fact, nearly everything must be purified with blood, and without the shedding of blood there is no forgiveness" Hebrews 9:22. Because of sin, the light wind life relationship in man that kept him alive was supplemented by the red fluid whom Christ Himself obtained when He came in the form of man. "For the life of the flesh *is* in the blood, and I have given it to you upon the altar to make atonement for your souls; for it *is* the blood *that* makes atonement for the soul" Leviticus 17:11; 14.

As we see later in the book, this concept was carried out literally by Pagan cultures. The actual interpretation of this scripture was reflecting Christ's suffering (persecution), death and resurrection and how He gave His Life that we might life to atone for this sin of Adam and Eve in the Garden of Eden.

"There are three things that are too wonderful for me yea four things that I know not (do not understand)" the writer said in Proverbs in Proverb 30:18, "The way of an eagle in the air; the way of a serpent upon a rock; the way of a ship in the midst of the sea; and the way of a man with a maid" v. 19. I say the latter rather than the former have yet to be deciphered. This is the Ultimate Image of God which is the image that reflects His character, HIMSELF, His Love, and what or who comes out of it; the ying and the yang of HIS PERSON. The fusion of two independent brains, hearts, bodies, and spirits to the ONENESS of HIM is what's uncompromisingly unfathomable. It digs deeper into understanding HIM as a Person to understand how to maneuver it and why so many have failed because they have neglected HIS PERSON and forged marriage into their own image not understanding a marriage without the acknowledgement or mirroring its origin is bound to fail. Unconditional love is obtained by observing and emulating HIM. It is HIS EXPRESS IMAGE, yet independent of each other being of One Mind, yet presenting different attributes and characteristics. Utterly amazing!

There is no illustration of love in the bible that reflects the undying and relentless characteristic of love that 1 Corinthians 13:1-3. It eliminates any indication of clauses or conditions to this law of love. I want to call it a law because it is a command and without it, life would be lifeless and life cannot exist without it or HIM. It reads, "Though I speak with the tongues of men and of angels, but have not love, I have become sounding brass or a clanging cymbal. And though I have the gift of prophecy, and understand all mysteries and all knowledge, and though I have all faith, so that I could remove mountains, but have not love, I am nothing. And though I bestow all my goods to feed the poor, and though I give my body to be burned, but have not love, it profits me nothing."

All the efforts we exert on the body to express ourselves, is nothing if love is excluded. If we burn ourselves through lust or literal cremation, if we confess Christ and/or any other deity and perform all the duties that exemplify charity and humility against love is considered useless. Another portion of scripture states that we can love God all we want but if we hate our neighbors, brothers etc. then we lie and the love of God is not in us; 1 John 4:20. "If a man says, I love God, and hate his brother, he is a liar: for he that loves not his brother whom he has seen, how can he love God whom he has not seen?"

The bible and other religious books have dedicated to the ideology and existence of love because of the recognition of its importance and significance for everyday living. It is first expressed and exists between family relations and spreads out like a tree covering others who happen to be plugged in to this tree that first began with the family unit. I refer to those others as extended family members, friends, co-workers etc. Anything that stems out of the family and affects or is touched by its branches whether due to work relations, business associations, church affiliations etc. anything that touches you is included. Societies that flourish are those that exercise the laws of love: Law because of its importance for sustenance and endurance. It is a must that love be instituted in our day to day life with the golden rule in effect. Alternative to the Golden Rule is the platinum rule created and used in human resources arena states "Treat others the way they want to be treated."

It all boils down to the law of reciprocity. We know that God is not mocked and whatsoever a man sows so shall he reap. It's Karma; it's everything that defines how we see ourselves and others.

In the beginning, John 1:1 it is written the ultimate lover of our souls that existed then in WORD form, as the author and orchestrator and designer of ourselves, loved us so much HE expressed HIMSELF in and through HIS creation by creating a form and image of HIS OWN SELF. Man reflects ELOHIM as the Jews call HIM. We are HIS little pieces. He basically created HIMSELF as he expressed HIMSELF through us and then in John 1:14 He extended HIS ultimate expression of HIMSELF and LOVE and became literally one of us. He picked a time, a place and a people to identify HIMSELF with HIS OWN SELF illustrated in us; HIS little people. An extension of heavenly things was expressed to earthly things. He expressed HIS dominance and most of HIS LOVE as undying and continuous by being one of HIS own ultimate creatures.

This is by far the most powerful. The most powerful creation stories rooted in LOVE became the most powerful LOVE stories ever written. He could not leave us to be condemned in the curse he spoke against yet became in order to redeem us from it. HE was from the beginning, the Letter of the Law; which was designed for those that fell i.e. Lucifer and the third (3rd) of fallen angels. We adopted the law when we became a part of the fallen through disobedience and evil alliances that produced evil. An alliance with evil was considered evil much like being charged with an accessory to something committed in a court of law.

Being the Law and the Letter, having spoken the curse because of His status as the Law and Letter of the Law, came down from His dwelling became that which He condemned in order to win us back again. John 1:14; the WORD (Letter, Law) became flesh and blood if I might add and .. "dwelt among us, and we beheld His glory, the glory as of the only begotten of the Father, full of grace and truth." I find that profound. His undying Love for us pursued us with such affection to the point of death; even though death could not hold him. He took charge of it all and sent it where it belonged; the underworld. This would be the most practical illustration of His undying love and affection that we ought to exercise on a day to day basis.

There cannot be a duplicate of the events displayed in HIS birth, Life, Death and Resurrection. Even though scientifically under the right circumstances a man can be brought back to life, there can never be another LOVE. He is the ultimate and sole LOVE and because of it, it extends unrestrained, unrestricted and is unrelenting; Life without end or should I say Love without end.

2 Corinthians 3:4-6 "And we have such trust through Christ toward God. Not that we are sufficient of ourselves to think of anything as being from ourselves, but our sufficiency is from God, who also made us sufficient as ministers of the new covenant, *not of the letter but of the Spirit; for the letter kills, but the Spirit gives life.*"

The Letter (Law, WORD) which destroyed us because of our inability to contain it, ushered in a new constitution, the SPIRIT of the LETTER which sustained us. Highlight on Grace who is the SPIRIT of the LETTER that was given on the day of Pentecost while the 120 waited which will usher in the next chapter of this book in great detail. Grace who is often portrayed us a virtue versus an actual PERSON extended this undying Love not that the first was on default but because we couldn't live up to the Law and condemned ourselves by our incomplete living. The term Grace of God is the actual expression of the PERSON of GOD who extends this LOVE LIFE we were ordered to be to live. He is the FAVOR, the BLESSING the LIFE of Christ that was given to GOD lovers.

In grave detail, the dispensation of Grace is dispensation of the Holy Ghost Himself. When you Grace of God you're saying Holy Spirit of God, the Enabler, the Helper, the Comforter, the Everything, very present Help, the Blessed Blesser, originator of Favor and why we receive Favor.

But I understand how confusing it is. Grace is the PERSON, the LAW instituted or introduced, Grace is God Himself, is no mess, and cannot be insulted. Matthew 12:31 reads "So I tell you, every sin and blasphemy can be forgiven--except blasphemy against the Holy Spirit, which will never be forgiven." Face like flint in Isaiah 50:7 depicts the One who lifts it up; Psalm 3:3, Nehemiah 8:10 Joy and Strength.

So therefore, when Grace is "hidden" or countenance "falls" judgment falls! Psalm 30:7 records "LORD, by thy favor thou hast made my mountain to stand strong: thou didst hide thy face, and I was troubled" The Law and the Letter were imparted when Grace was hidden and when the Letter of the Law was and is instituted, judgment falls. Judgment is the extension of HIS WRATH and condemnation for breaking the Letter of the LAW; breaking HIM literally and He; GRACE retracts and THE LAW reacts in WRATH by oracles that come from the LAW HIMSELF. We cannot win breaking LETTER LAW WORD, He is ALPOWERFUL and we mere dust into which we return since out of it we came.

Hebrews 6:1-8 emphasis on Verse 6 records, "Therefore, leaving the discussion of the elementary principles of Christ, let us go on to perfection, not laying again the foundation of repentance from dead works and of faith toward God, of the doctrine of baptisms, of laying on of hands, of resurrection of the dead, and of eternal judgment. And this we will do if God permits. For it is impossible for those who were once enlightened, and have tasted the heavenly gift, and have become partakers of the Holy Spirit, and have tasted the good word of God and the powers of the age to come, if they fall away, to renew them again to repentance, _since they crucify again for themselves the Son of God, and put Him to an open shame_. For the earth which drinks in the rain that often comes upon it, and bears herbs useful for those by whom it is cultivated, receives blessing from God; but if it bears thorns and briers, it is rejected and near to being cursed, whose end is to be burned.

Clearly rebellion; the sin of witchcraft (1 Samuel 15:23), which is of non-effect against HIS OWN (Numbers 23:23), brings about the utterance of death and condemnation which takes place because HE (LETTER LAW WORD) exists and is real.

Psalm 104:29 "Thou hidest thy face, they are troubled: thou takest away their breath, they die, and return to their dust." I'm keeping thy face, Thee Grace! He's the peace that passes ALL understanding, the Keeper of the *heart and *mind, in Christ. He is the Lifter up of thine and mine's head.

8

The Waiting Game

PATIENCE PAYS IN PROPHESY; PERFECT
TIMING PRODUCES PERFECT WILL

Good things come to those who wait for sure. And at other times failing to recognize one's blessing or visitation can be fatal. "In the fullness of time, or but when the fullness of time was come, God sent forth His Son, made of a woman, made under the law..." Galatians 4:4 is an express indication that God has His own timing and waiting brought about the perfect will of God. On the contrary, Luke 19:44 explains the consequences of missing the perfect moment. Jesus was the consolation of Israel and a vast majority of Israel was blinded by ignorance; having read and taught the writings of the prophets; the scriptures, they were still blinded by the ideologies and structure of man. They expected a King wearing royal robes and not swaddling clothes making it impossible to accept their true King who neither came wearing royal robes, nor administratively commanded an army to overthrow Rome. Their blind ambition caused them to miss their moment which brought about consequences that followed.

Between Genesis 3 when the messiah was promised and Matthew 1 when conception took place between God the Holy Spirit and Mary was several, (approximately) four thousand years. A day to the Lord is a thousand years to man. The heavenly - galactic calendar doesn't operate earthly calendar. In explaining the end times and the affairs that took place explaining prophesy also reflects the conflict and disagreement between heaven's timing and earth's interpretation of that timing.

We've waited and continue to wait. According to the Jewish calendar which dates back to the time when man acknowledged with his own mouth to be 5778 when this book was first written. Which means we're almost at the 6000th year mark which will usher in the 1000-year reign of peace according to prophesy where Satan will be bound and Christ and His people will reign.

The mankind road to freedom hasn't been easy. It began with a woman and it'll end with figurative image of a woman where the two will finally bruise and crush each other. The bruising has been taking place so has the crushing of the head been gradual. God again isn't bound by time as we know it so 2 Peter 3:8 and Psalm 90:4 explain we've only been here almost 6 days.

Empires have been forged from as we remember it from scripture the Nimrodians, who preceded the Egyptians; the Pharaohs (1570BCE - 1069BCE) then came the Assyrians (2334BC to 2154BC - Middle Assyrian Empire 1392BC – 1056BC then Neo Assyrian empire from 911BC and 609BC), the Babylonian's Nebuchadnezzar (Image of head of Gold – Daniel 2 and the Lion in Daniel 7 -from 605BC to 539BC), then Medo-Persians' Darius and Cyrus (silver chest in Daniel 2 and Bear in Daniel 7, also the Ram in Daniel 8 – from 539BC - 331BC) and then came the Greek's Alexander the Great (the bronze skirt in Daniel 2 and leopard in Daniel 7 and the he goat in Daniel 8. The he goat's horn was broken and from it came up four notable ones toward the four winds of heaven which were represented by the four generals who ruled Asia Minor under **Lysimachus**, Egypt, Palestine, Cilicia, Petra and Cyprus under **Ptolemy I**. He founded the Ptolemaic Dynasty which lasted until the death of Cleopatra VII in 30 BCE, Mesopotamia to India ruled by **Seleucus I Nicator**, and **Cassander** who controlled Macedonia and Greece, after Alexander the Great from 7331BC – 168BC).

The Republic of Rome (Iron legs in Daniel 2 and mystery fourth beast, was terrifying, frightening and very powerful. It had large iron teeth; it crushed and devoured its victims and trampled underfoot whatever was left in Daniel 7 from 168BC – 476AD). Papal Rome reigned from 476AD to 533AD) and after that the ascension of Papal Rome as a reigning empire took hold in 534AD where the capitals were relocated from Constantinople under Constantine, the Byzantine thereby naming it the Byzantine Empire. Having been intercepted by THE one-eyed African Queen and her three other surrounding female monarch friends of her region from 40BC to 10AD after Cleopatra died by venom, her and her armies defined Roman's status of invasion into the entire African continent; Rome was confined to its European territories as a result a forging a peace treaty with the African Queens led by Amanirenat aka Queen Candace. I'll try and keep it short to keep myself from getting confused with the timelines.

Meanwhile the 10 horns made up of Western Europeans which disintegrated the Roman empire (***Lombards***) and broke apart into the 10 toes in Daniel 2 which also were referred to the 10 horns or the 10 tribes which later being led by the modern Lion i.e. Great Britain (***Anglo-saxons***) and then France (***Franks***) and the Spain (***Visigoths***), all these attempting to unite together, work together by intermarrying within their monarchs, but couldn't because the clay and the iron in Daniel's image (Daniel 2), were mingled together therefore disintegrated into different groups. Prior to Great Britain taking root, from the Moors (Barbarians, along with the ***Vandals*** who were also a part of the 10 toes) under Muhammad, 622AD – 632AD under Rashidun caliphs, 632AD – 661AD and under Umayyad caliphs, 661AD – 750AD who conquered the Visigoth's in 711AD and Ottoman Turks (from 1299AD - 1922AD), the Moors -The Barbarians, the Ottoman Turks, the Africans and the Arabs ruled Europe for a while. The other unnamed 10 tribes of the Roman Empire which made up Western Europe also included the ***Ostrogoths, Heruli, Suevi, Burgundi*** and ***Alamani.***

Papal Rome ascended from 534AD to 1798AD. Christianity was legalized much earlier under Constantine who was originally a Republic Ruler, from 306AD and 337AD. The pact Constantine put in place protecting Christians from persecution was done away with in 534AD, giving Papal Rome the absolute power to persecute Protestants as they saw fit. Constantine is perhaps best known for being the first Christian Roman emperor. His rule changed the Church greatly. In February 313AD, Constantine met with Licinius in Milan where they made the Edict of Milan. The edict said that Christians could believe what they wanted.

At the Council of Niacea, under Constantine, some of the Protestant Clergymen; Bishops in 325AD are said to have sat down at the Canon assembly with bruises and scars. Some were limping; others had missing limbs and body parts by mutilation. Europe and its surroundings are said to have been a very dark place in history which is why Constantine was prompted to abolish persecution of Christian much earlier after his miraculous conversion brought about by the vision he had. His conversion was said to be peculiar. Having been in a trance or otherwise, Constantine saw a vision of a cross made by the sun's reflection creating the cross and a voice following instructing him that by that sign of the cross created by the sun's reflections/rays/light, he would defeat the Roman Republic.

Persecution of the Christians is said to have begun around 34AD with the stoning of Steven after Christ's ascension into heaven. Paul the apostle was one of the persecutors and perpetrators of this persecution. Republic of Rome permitted the instigation from the High Priests of Roman Israel because they were threatened by this new ideology the Christ whom the saw, ate, talked, and walked with was GOD. It was blasphemy and they sought to overthrow Him and His regime. Republic of Rome however under the first Herod didn't want any competition; a threat to his own kingdom, sought to slay the Child Christ as he fled into Egypt where he remained hidden until King Herod died. I am reiterating that, Queen Candace/Amanirenat, the one eyed Cushite Queen, made his hiding possible to stopping Roman invasion into Egypt and beyond.

So, between 534BC to 1798AD ***the woman with the 12 stars in revelation 12*** was "given wings" when the dragon sought after the Child she brought forth, and fled into the wilderness where she was nourished 1260 years. If you do the math, it was 1260 years the dark ages presented darkness and persecution of Christians from Papal Powers of Rome up until 1798 when Napoleon seized the Pope and banished him to exile until his death 6 weeks later.

Remembering a day to the Lord is as a 1000 years, the understanding the a time, 2 times and half a time is equal to three and a half years which made up the 1260 days which have been translated by the events and the duration of the events to be the time of Jacob's trouble characterized by the scriptural reference below. Ref: Revelation 11:3 "*and **I will give power unto my two witnesses, and they shall prophecy a thousand two hundred and sixty days, clothed in sackcloth**.*" This is indeed speculator but fitting understanding the origin of the persecutor and what they have represented since. Mary, "the mother of God" is worshipped instead of Christ. This is the symbol of the great whore of Babylon (who converted the entire continent), made them drank with her whoredoms (understanding spiritual infidelity and idolatry to which Virgin Mary represents, is equal to adultery and/or harlotry).

In Pagan Rome idolatry was prevalent so it was easy for Mary the mother of Christ to be adopted into Roman beliefs as a deity, which is happening to this day. Jesus never referred to her as a god in any way but indoctrinations from prior religious beliefs did among the Romans. It's blasphemy according to scripture as we are instructed and commanded not to have any other gods before, besides, above or beneath HIM, Exodus 20:3-5. He is the only One true and wise GOD. "'Hear, O Israel: The Lord our God, the Lord is one" Deuteronomy 6:4; Mark 12:29. And we are to "love HIM, your God with all your heart and with all your soul and with all your strength" v.5, v.30. This absolute Love for God will keep us devoted and faithful from following after another that isn't God; much like a marriage covenant. Can't love two masters; either you'll love one and hate the other etc. Matthew 6:24.

DANIEL 7:25

"He shall speak great words against the Most-High, and shall wear out the saints of the Most-High, and think to change times and laws -- and they shall be given into his hands until a time and times and the dividing of a time." They did. The laws that were changed included but not limited to the Sabbath law. Constantine authorized and sealed the gathering together of the Saints on which the Christians, even Christ Himself and Christians up until this point where the change took place from Saturday to Sunday, making Sunday the day of rest. Saturday is the Lord's Sabbath and ought to be observed as the Holiest Day of rest.

Some argue that Paul preached into the 1ˢᵗ day of the week which was s Sunday. They omit the fact that his sermon began on the Sabbath and continued on to the 1ˢᵗ day of the week which was the Sabbath upon which the young man fell three stories high from exhaustion Acts 20:9.

Some might argue the day of Pentecost was the 1ˢᵗ day of the week. Yes. The apostles were accustomed to gathering; in fact, they were kept hidden due to persecution and were instructed not to leave until the comforter was sent. He indeed came the 50ᵗʰ day the feast of Jubilee which happened to be the 1ˢᵗ day of the week. 7 weeks had passed during the feast of Jubilee after Passover and on the day of Pentecost, the Holy Ghost was sent.

Paganism was prevalent in those days and the sun a deity. Constantine's vision may have contributed to this change as in those days the sun was worshipped and since the sign of the cross made by the sun promised him victory, so did the day of worship followed soon after to commemorate the sun.

"Remember the Sabbath day, to keep it holy" (Exodus 20:8). Many promises and blessings are extended to those who keep the law of the Sabbath. For example, in the days of Jeremiah, the Lord promised to spare Jerusalem and its inhabitants if they would keep the Sabbath (see Jeremiah 17:20–27). In our day the Lord has promised us the "fullness of the earth" if we will obey this commandment

Others are stuck on this notion; Jesus resurrected on the 1ˢᵗ day of the week making it Holy overlooking the resurrection could not have taken place in the Sabbath since that would break the rest law. If Jesus were to resurrect on the Sabbath, then work would be legalized on the Sabbath as the Holy Spirit Himself would have initiated in the resurrection of Christ on the Sabbath, having broken the rest law for the Sabbath. He had to be resurrected on the 1ˢᵗ day of the week and remained rested on the Sabbath.

All in all, the three Monotheistic religions, all commemorate the persecution of Christ, His death, burial and His resurrection whether we like it or not. God does have a sense of humor. These three Monotheistic establishments rooted in Abraham, neither agrees, affirm, nor commune with one another, yet confirm His Life, His work, His way and His Love, separately. "The Moors" commune on Friday, The 7ᵗʰ days and The Jews on the Sabbath and the rest of the Church on Sunday.

Christ said, He will build His Church, HE DID and the gates of hades will not prevail against it, even if the war originates from within as it has since its birth.

DANIEL 12:7

"It shall be for a time, times, and half a time that he can scatter the power of the holy people." This was described as and marked with the entry of the dark ages 534AD – 1798AD, when the church entered an era of persecution. The church is said to have scattered hence the term Jews and/or Christians in diaspora where Christians went into hiding from the face of the perpetrators. The edict that was signed and passed by Constantine some 200 years prior was broken leaving Christians vulnerable and open to blatant assault as they kept their faith.

REVELATION 11:2

"The holy city they tread under foot forty and two months." The Church was trod upon by Papal powers. Pope declared himself the one and only true Vicar of God on earth, disseminating all else as heretics thereby killing and causing destruction to believers of Christ. This was during the dark ages when persecution of Christians was prevalent for 42 months also characterized by 3 and half years which translates to 1260 years with Papal's inception of persecution of Christians

REVELATION 12:6

"And the woman fled into the wilderness, where she hath a place prepared by God that they should feed her there a thousand two hundred and sixty days." This was marked by the church going into hiding to survive persecution from the Pope and Papal reign and by the commencement of the broken covenant to allow Christians to worship God freely and revealing of the dragon which was symbolized by Papal Rome's perception. He was the ten toes which were part iron and part clay Daniel 2

REVELATION 12:14

"And the woman was given wings of a great eagle that she might fly into the wilderness, where she is nourished for a time, and times, and half a time, from the face of the serpent." The church ran into hiding, scattered upon the face of the earth from the serpent and dragon which meant the same devilish destructive figure who sought to destroy the true church of Christ thereby destroying Christ Himself based on the ideology behind its persecutory acts.

REVELATION 13:5

"And there was given to the beast a mouth speaking great things and blasphemies, and power was given to him to continue forty and two months." The beast, the religious authoritative figure that exalted himself against the knowledge of God declaring himself to be god on earth during those times, deciding who was to live or who was to die, writing and passing laws contrary to the Commandments of God.

The Revelation of Jesus Christ by John the revelator is about just that. His revealing when all will see him return for his bride, the church. The Holy Spirit who is not to be blasphemed or insulted is aiding our wait, though it seems long will surely come. And we shall not only behold him but ascend into heaven as we (those of that time) saw Him leave. The story of mankind has been a Love story. God Loves us so much that HE not only reproduced His own self not realizing who we (Adam and Eve) were, sinned and even in that Love, He never abandoned us because of His Great Love for us. While we were yet sinners, Christ returned to the earth that He had cursed because of the sin that produced an illegitimate child Cain. He returned legitimately to seize the power from whom it was given at the garden and restored our fellowship, authority, and place in this life and the life to come. As Cain was Eve's first born conceived of a spirit; who hadn't been touched by Adam yet so did Jesus return of a woman who hadn't been touched by Joseph yet. I call that legitimizing illegitimacy.

In the story of Noah, Satan also tried to pollute every woman that lived with his fallen angels to keep Christ from being housed in a Holy womb. Christ fixed that in that the fallen angels are no longer appealing to the eye due to the deformities they received in battle camouflaged by the 40 day and 40 night rainfall which flooded the earth; a merely a shadow of what was going on behind the scenes whereby a war in the heavenliest ensured the demolition and utter demise of the fallen angels so that when a woman would look upon a fallen angel, she would flee in fright at the hideous appearance and not be seduced by his angelic looks.

God made sure that reproduction was as He commanded, after His Likeness by deforming fallen angels. Christ did that to protect her. It may sound folkish but look at what happened next. No record of demons or should I say, fallen angels mating with the daughters of men have been reported. His plan and will came to fruition and at the fullness of time, God was conceived of the Holy Spirit in a woman's body; the womb-man carried God to fruition and birthed Him and the curse was lifted since God walked on this earth since birth to manhood.

It's always been about the Seed of the woman:

The iron and clay mixture of the ten toes is depicted in today's Europe; the European Union losing the UK via Brexit. The book of Daniel 2:41-43 "and whereas thou sawest the feet and toes, part of potters' clay, and part of iron, the kingdom shall be divided; but there shall be in it of the strength of the iron, forasmuch as thou sawest the iron mixed with miry clay. And as the toes of the feet were part of iron, and part of clay, so the kingdom shall be partly strong, and partly broken? And whereas thou sawest iron mixed with miry clay, ***_they" shall mingle themselves with "the seed of men:_*** " (sons of Adam), but they shall not cleave one to another, even as iron is not mixed with clay." It is in fact the man who bears seed – catchy.

I'm deliberately referring to the differences between the Sons of God and Daughters of Men Reference: Job 1:6 sons of God presenting themselves before God and Satan came also with them. Daughters of men reference from Genesis 6:4 to paint a picture of Anno Domini's Europe and Africa. The seed of men in Daniel 2:43 refers to the Adamic sons (the red/brown/black ones) while "they" in scripture refers to the daughters of God (the white ones) being taken, giving themselves or being given to the seed of men to mingle the seed; a portrayal of unity through lineage and breeding for population.

Daniel 2:41-43 and the "mingling with the "seed of men;" a representation of the unifying of kingdoms and peoples of a different race either by intermarrying as the kingdoms of Europe did when princes and princesses, kings and queens married into each other's families, so did this mingling will and has been taking place. This enhances the various families (empires and kingdoms) to coexist on a peaceful front. Let's not forget the Vandals settlement in the continent of Africa in the Northern side.

I mentioned earlier the peace treaty forged by the African Cushite Queen Amanirenat and Europe via Rome, not only enhanced the peaceful coexistence between the "sons of God" and the "seed of men" but also weakened Roman influence over the continent they never conquered. Soon after, the Moors sought to rule over Europe which ultimately led to the Transatlantic. I believe there can't be one without the other as they are intertwined with chain of events. For example, an opportunity presented itself for workers to till the "newfoundland" which was "found" by Christopher Columbus thanks to the Spanish inquisition which research reveals got the voyage route to the Americas by the Moors who were already voyaging abroad to the Americas from Europe and Africa. The 14th Century Spanish inquisition led by King Charles V and Queen Isabella after seizing Spain from the Moors, led to the Jews and Moors to be displaced. The Moors simply returned to their land in Africa, and Asia but mostly Africa. The Jews however became displaced creating the need to find land for their occupation hence the Trans Atlantic slave trade.

Over time and 400 years later the "seed of men" have fought to be completely free but it wasn't until the 400th anniversary that another treaty was signed commemorating the 400-year occupation of Africans in the Americans. The Africans of the Americans according to migration routes tracks back into Israel. The lost tribes and other displaced peoples, thanks to General Titus at 70AD, where Christ prophesied their displacement in Matthew 23 and the many other times Israel has been displaced due to persecution of dominating empires of the past and present. The fact of the matter is, the mingling with the seed of men that has taken place since Cain and Abel and more so now with territories establishing who gets to occupy where clearly paints a picture of attempted unification between the races which will not completely pen out because of political agendas, and the conceited desire to exploit resources, flush out melanin off the face of the earth with white supremacists seeking absolute control of the world. These agenda is leading the new world order all because of the difference in appearance.

This new world order will trigger the Christ Himself to establish His eternal Kingdom prompting Him to rule with a fist of iron preventing history from repeating itself. Reason why the threat looms is because man was created with a free spirit and free will which has tended to destroy the good but the fact that Satan will be forever quarantined will make eternal Peace a reality. He'll be completely disabled from enticing the human race into violating the way therefore leading man to violence. Violations of God leads to violence and displacements; I'm not excluding Brexit and the effort for the ten toes to unite i.e. the clay and iron with France calling for a European military but God will not allow it, thanks to the migration crisis of 2014 and beyond with Germany's Merkel *(one of "they"),* letting in over a million African refugees (majority of the Moorish belief system) to aid population which has been on the decline. The depletion of population in Europe is a big factor to the "mingling with seed of men" (blending in with the population of the peoples of the Adamic race); with the continuing of the seed/people, culture, values, beliefs and way of life as a whole to promote tolerance, and enhance the population. Diversity is becoming more and more appealing even with the sons and daughters of God. Peace through cooperation and unification to bring about prosperity and advancement, which is the current state of affairs. Enhancing this peace and security for advancement into the one world system is anticipated more and more as the younger generations uphold this diversity of the human race.

Agenda: Just as Nimrod ascribed to himself with the unification of the known world and attempted to build the tower of Babel so that they could be forever one, crediting his own achievements; (as Lucifer seeking to overthrow or at least attempt to reach where God was), so will the New world. Just as Nimrod's world was brought to confusion so will the new world. The human race will seek diversity and become as one giving credit only to their own achievements, seeking to modify what God created (DNA modifications, cloning and other achievements), having their own agenda, then crediting it to their own selves excluding the Creator of this Universe just as Lucifer did. What is hidden will be revealed. The mastermind behind the New World Order has never been to acknowledgement the God of the Universe but another and thus it'll not stand. The Rock cut out without hands will bring it to naught and Christ will establish His own eternal Kingdom; thwarting His opponents.

The last of the events is what we're all looking forwards to: "the Rock cut out without hands," crushing the image all together and a strong new mountain appearing in its stead in Daniel 2:34-45. The ten toes made of clay and iron were the last human kingdom that has prevailed for centuries; out of which the "entire earth have been made drunk with its wine" and partaken in its idolatries.

Part of the reason or the main reason why the gentiles were so open to receiving the message of Christ was because those Pagan societies were accustomed to having gods for just about everything and anything. Another "God' added to their list was going to be beneficial for them. A God who forgave sins, healed the sick, raised the dead, walked on water, fed 5000, cast out devils; basically performed every miracle imaginable was a welcome into their culture; only if they could control and where agendas are born and Christ shows Himself strong. The passages following are research supporting the concept that the Pagan

world embraced another deity and likened Christ to the others but He was far Greater, He was God in the flesh. This was and has always been the work of Satan to pervert the truth and "ascend into or above the heights of the clouds; and be like the most High" Isaiah 14:14

For Example: (Replacement Theology)

The story of Mary and her virgin birth of Christ was likened to **Osiris – EGYPT:** He came to fulfill the law. Called "KRST," the "Anointed One" born of the virgin Isis-Meri on December 25th in a cave / manger, with his birth announced by a star and attended by three wise men. His earthly father was named "Seb" (which translates to "Joseph.") At age 12 he was a child teacher in the Temple and at 30 he was baptized, having disappeared for 18 years. Osiris was baptized in the river Iarutana -- the river Jordan -- by "Anup the Baptizer," who was beheaded. (Anup translates to John.) He performed miracles, exorcised demons, raised El-Osiris from the dead. Walked on water and was betrayed by Typhon, crucified between two thieves on the 17th day of the month of Athyr. Buried in a tomb from which he arose on the third day (19th Athyr) and was resurrected. His suffering, death, and resurrection celebrated each year by His disciples on the Vernal Equinox -- Easter. Called "The Way, the Truth, the Light," "Messiah," "god's Anointed Son,' the "Son of Man," the "Word made Flesh," the "word of truth" is expected to reign a thousand years.

Around the 18th-19th dynasties in Egypt when Israel inhabited Egypt, the Exodus I believe not only was accompanied by the "mixed multitude" who were of Egyptian ancestry but there were those of Israel tribe who remained and hence these comparisons between the myths and truth. Mark and Philip apostleship led evangelism to these "lost tribes' of the house of Israel, who Christ not only fled to but many of the Israelites throughout history took refuge in for centuries before and centuries after Christ. Egypt's geographical location neighboring Israel put their relationship to be seen as sibling nations e.g. Ephraim and Manasseh being the two Egyptian tribes that make up the nation of Israel, with Ishmael's mother Hager, being an Egyptian. It wouldn't be surprising to find written manuscripts overlapping and pouring into neighboring borders.

Second deity recorded is Mithra. ***The story of Christ was foretold in many of these neighboring nations and regions prompting Christ to "disappear" to these regions of India and surrounding Asiatic regions after the age of 12 for the next 18 years of his missing years until He turned up at 30 and as the Prophet Isaiah, even King David prophesied*** *of His coming. It isn't surprising these stories were foretold by their seers (unknown-by observing God protocol of bringing tidings throughout scripture), prophesying He too would tread their lands.* Whether Satan could interpret prophesies or was even aware of God's plan of impregnating a virgin girl to bring forth Christ the Son of God who referred to Himself as Son of Man is sure. Mithras was a Persian deity. He was the expansively acclaimed god in the Roman Empire during the inception of the Christ we call Jesus. His existence during Papal times caused quite a stir as his existence was not acceptable but tolerated. This deity was passed down and it was up to the Jewish religious leaders to upset its present by replacing their belief in the idol by the One True Messiah, Papal leaders instead of completely wiping Mithras existence out, borrowed some of its theories, baptizing them into Christianity, creating a parallel of beliefs between the two religions. Where you find the similarities therein:

1) Three Wise Men of Persia, hundreds of years before Christ for example, came to visit the baby savior-god Mithra, bringing him gifts of gold, myrrh and frankincense.

2) Mithra was said to have been born on December 25 as told in the "Great Religions of the World", page 330; "…it was the winter solstice that celebrated his birth by ancients of Mithraism's sun god." Nimrod in ancient texts is said to have fathered "the sun" by his mother, giving birth to the sun worship idea. Mithra could or could not have had another name sun -"Rah" but this I cannot prove. The similarities could be coincidental or Mithra carried on a second identity.

3) The 12 signs of the Zodiac represent the 12 followers called "disciples" whom Mithra had and who he ate with at the last supper prior to him being crucified on the cross.

4) Upon Mithra's death, his body was laid in a tomb which was a cave rock.

5) Mithra too practiced celibacy and thus was his priesthood.

6) Mithra ascended at spring (Passover) equinox when the sun and the equator cross paths, making night and day of equal to each other in length.

Whether by ancient prophesy Christ was foretold in these ancient Pagan societies, as the Bible foretold His coming or whether the similarities were indeed coincidental with the attempt to replace an old wives fable replacing the true with the deceit or whether Papal clergies sought absolute power by replacing their already accepted norm and form with this newly evidently powerful force isn't clear but comparing Jewish writings from eye witness followers, we know that the latter was a threat to the former which needed ousting but in order to maintain customs, one had to look as the other.

So we see here how Christianity derived many of its essential elements from the ancient religion of Mithraism, which could or couldn't be ancient pagan prophesies of the coming Messiah. Mithraism became intertwined with the "cult of Jesus" which happens to be the other way around the cult of Mithraism to expand what is known today as "Christianity." In spite of the fact that mythical sources on Mithraic cult religion are rare, plenty of evidentiary material exists in a lot of Mithraic temples which were typically underground carved caves filled with an exceptionally intricate iconography; illustrations by pictures, figures and images, and relics archaeologists discovered dispersed throughout the Empire of Rome, to England in the north to the west to Palestine in the south and east.

We often hear about how the traditions, rites and symbols of modern day "Christianity" with its holidays are rooted in paganism. For example the much celebrated December 25th which was chosen to celebrate the birth of Jesus? If I was allowed to correct this selection of his birth and reflect that Jesus Christ was in fact the Lamb of God. Anyone who rears sheep/lamps understand that Lamps are born at the beginning of Spring; a discovery Prophet Joanthan Cann made as he sought to bring light to truth. This could only mean Christ being the first born from the dead (Colossians 1:18), was actually born in March 21st. It is not a coincident, Papal powers sought control and were threatened by this new King of the Jews that ancient paganism and the story of Mithras' birth just happens to coincide with the Christmas time. Around the time of the birth of the Lambs is when shepherds would have been "tending their flocks in the field" and the new lambs were born. Strange enough, the ancient pagan religion, Mithraism, which dates back over 4,000 years, also celebrated the birth of their "savior" on December 25th. This could have been revealed by some "deity" who understood times and seasons straight out of Jewish prophesies.

Franz Cumont, a leading research expert on Roman Paganism, clarified the ancient religion entitled Mithraism that:

"Mithras was said to have returned to earth to impart people His instructions and begin Secrets and rituals which would aid humans recall His acts on our behalf. Because of His works, we can choose to be and do good without the overpowering influence of evil, even though evil's effect can still seem prevailing because our minds believe it is. Due to His teachings, we understand our purpose in life is to serve others in the name of Mithras. The followers refer to Him as the *"Light of the World"* a phrase often used in Christian faith when referring to Jesus.

Philo of Alexandria (30 BCE - 45 CE), cautioned against this prevalent credulous acceptance in coming together between male gods and human females. The offspring's are known as demigods. This son of a god born of a virgin ideology, belief and practice, was so widespread in those days that Tammuz, who was assimilated into Attis and Mithras, emulated the story in the New Testament bible, because these were all deities who were supposed to have died and resurrected. Tammuz was always referred to as Adon, which means Lord; (The Greek Adonis was based on him). In fact, these deities were based on the first divine being to have died and resurrected including the Egyptian god Osiris. So the only unique about Jesus is that He was not only the Only True Lord and God but that His coming was Prophesied, centuries prior making mimicking a possibility and I think He was "cloned" in all these deities through the foreknowledge of His pre-existence from Prophesy;

Of these deities, folklores and myths spread that they were indeed born of a virgin; cloned the divine nature and story of the True Messiah.

Below are some of the clones of past centuries widely believed as the gods who cloned Christ.

Augustus (his father was the god Apollo)	Agdistis	Attis
Adonis	Buddha	Dionysus
Korybas	Krishna	Mithras
Osirus	Perseus	Romulus and Remus
Tammuz	Zoroaster	Jesus

So, all the pagan religions of times past were not only alike, but cloned to emulate Christianity. It just so happens only one of them got the preeminence, and became the most influential, wiping out all others. In addition to a lack of chronological evidence, many physiognomies of Christ, which Christians today believe in, are irrefutably similar or identical to beliefs and dogmas that heralded Christianity. There several versions of pagan gods of rather different cultures who were said to have had the same qualities as those of Christians claim Jesus possessed leading to confusion and every evil work (James 3:16) but more so inquiries regarding the origin of the Christian claim:

ATTIS - Phrygia: He was born of the virgin Nana on December 25th and was both the Father and the Divine Son; the savior. He was crucified on a tree for the salvation of world. He was buried and on the third day his clerics found his tomb empty -- He had risen from the dead (on March 25th). His supporters were baptized in blood, thereby washing away their sins -- after which were declared "born again." His followers ate a consecrated bread, which was believed became the body of their savoir.

BUDDIAH – INDIA: He too was born of a virgin Maya on December 25th, with his birth announced by a star and visited by wise men presenting exorbitant gifts. At his birth, the angels herald his birth and burst in song with heavenly songs. He taught in the temple at the age of 12. Tempted by Mara, the Evil One (Satan), while fasting and then baptized in the water and with the Spirit of God being present. Buddiah healed the sick, fed 500 from a small basket of cakes (Christ fed 5000), walked on water. He came to fulfill the law and preached the establishment of a kingdom of righteousness and obliged followers to poverty and to renounce worldly pleasures. He was transfigured on a mount, died on a cross, in some traditions, buried but rose again after tomb opened itself by supernatural powers. He ascended into heaven (Nirvana), and will return in latter days to judge the dead. Buddiah was called "Good Shepherd," "Carpenter," "Alpha and Omega," "Sin Bearer," "Master," "Light of the World," "Redeemer," etc. How compelling.

DIONYSUS - GREECE: Born of a virgin on December 25th, he was also placed in a manger after his birth. There was no room for him at the inn. He was a nomadic teacher who did many a miracles, one of which included turning water into wine. His followers ate hallowed meal which became the body of the god. He rose from the dead (naturally as his clone) on March 25th. He was recognized as the ram and lamb and was called "King of Kings," "Only Begotten Son," "Savior," "Redeemer," "Sin bearer," "Anointed One," the "Alpha and Omega."

HERACLES – GREECE: He was born during the winter equinox of a virgin who abstained from sexual activity with her until her god-begotten child was born and was sacrificed during the spring equinox. He too, was called a "Savior," "Only begotten," "Prince of Peace," "Son of Righteousness."

KRISHNA - INDIA: Krishna was born while his foster-father Nanda was in the city to pay his tax to the king (how convenient). His nativity heralded by a star, Krishna was born of the virgin Devaki in a cave, for a lack of vacant rooms in the region during the time of his birth and his birth was miraculously illuminated with herds of cattle tendering to his birth. King

Kansa, the reigning king, sought the life of the Indian Christ by ordering the carnage of all male children born during the same night at "Herod's reign." Krishna traveled widely, performing miracles -- raising the dead, healing lepers, the deaf and the blind. The crucified Krishna hanged on the cross, arms stretched out, penetrated by an arrow. Krishna finally dies, but descends into Hell and from the midst, He rises again on the third day and rises into Heaven. (The Gospel of Nicodemus tells of Jesus' descent into Hell.) His return is set on the last day to judge the quick and the dead. Krishna is also the second person of the Hindu trinity, coincidentally so.

OSIRIS – EGYPT: He was also born of a virgin Isis-Meri on December 25th in a cave or manger, his birth having been announced by a star and attended by three wise men. His mission was to fulfill the law; He Called "KRST," the "Anointed One" and his earthly father was named "Seb" (translates to "Joseph"). At the age of 12, he was a child teacher in the Temple and at 30 he was baptized, having disappeared for 18 years.

*Important to note again that this disappearance of Christ was revealed to Him having resorted to India and the Asiatic regions due to the fact that **Jewish parents of young girls would present their daughters as was custom for engagements. At the age of 12, young Jewish boys became suitors for young Jewish brides and were betrothed to be married later on in their lives yet Christ's mission was not to settle but to fulfill the call of God His father.***

Osiris was also baptized in the river Iarutana - which is the river Jordan by "Anup the Baptizer," who was beheaded. (Anup translates to John). He performed miracles, exorcised demons, raised El-Osiris from the dead. Walked on water and was betrayed by Typhon, crucified between two thieves on the 17th day of the month of Athyr. He was buried in a tomb from which he arose on the third day (19th Athyr) and was resurrected. His suffering, death, and resurrection celebrated each year by His disciples on the Vernal Equinox – Easter (Ishtar). He is also called "the Way, the Truth, the Light," "the Messiah," "god's Anointed Son,' the "Son of Man," the "Word made Flesh," (John 1:14) the "word of truth." (John 14:6 says Way, Truth, Life), and is expected to reign a thousand years (Revelation 20)."

Paul was supposedly born and raised in the city of Tarsus, a region in SE Asia-Minor (now called Turkey) where the Mithras religion and practice was prevalent. Biblical scholars suspect Paul, the author of 13 out of the 27 (maybe more) books of the New Testament, may have come under the Mithraic spell and influenced his writings; a myth I shun as unbelief of Christ's word, way and work. We can see profound kinship between Mithraism and Christianity as Christianity progressed into what it is today.

Because Mithraism was so popular in Rome; it is no wonder why the pagan Emperor Constantine, who believed in the sun god, Mithras, designated a certain day of the week to him i.e. Sunday, which means, *"the day of the sun,"* changing the Sabbath law; reference: "and think to change times and laws:" in Daniel 7:25 **as it was foretold by the Prophet Daniel.** The Book of Daniel gives clear internal dates such as "the third year of the reign of king Jehoiakim," (1:1), that is, **606 BCE**); "the second year of the reign of king Nebuchadnezzar," (2:1), that is, **603 BCE**); "the first year of Darius," (9:1), that is **522 BCE**); "in the third year of Cyrus," (10:1), that is **547 BCE** or perhaps **536 BCE**).

"Christian" faith concoction of pagan, Mithramic, Judeo/Christian teaching not by Divine design but by manipulation; Satan being its orchestrator since time began as we know it and the time of the fall of his reign from heaven with the third of the stars. I believe astrology had quite abit to do with all these predictions as well, as true prophesy sought to establish itself in mankind. This led to the confusing mix of theology that we have today within the "Christian" community. This apostasy from the original simple and plain teachings of Christ were accelerated by the persecutions and killings of any who tried to support the "old" ways and could suppose this solved the mystery of the "ungodly" marriage between Mithraism and the cult of Jesus. As it turns out, it was all for political convenience, thanks to Rome and its powers seeking absolute control of the true nature, work and theology of Christ! The Christianity we have today has almost no relation, to the "the original teachings of Jesus because of the Pagan influence of the Powers that controlled the world during that time. The image in Daniel 2:31-35 describes it well. The legs of iron and feet that were partly clay and partly iron is a true depiction of the gospel. It was "mingled" with external pressure to comply with its demands for absolute control. Clay could mean the true religion as described in James 1:27 and the true knowledge of Christ, His Person, His Words, Way and Works and the iron was the existing Pagan influences.

These theologies presented two Jesus' teachings: Jesus the Jew and Jesus the Gentile (the mingling with the iron and clay Daniel 2:33) supposing which one of the Christians would follow the epic journey of the 12 disciples commissioned to "go to all the world and preach the gospel" Mark 16:15 and going into "all of the world and make disciples" Matthew 28:19. The ex-pagan Constantine liked his Jesus over the Jesus of the Jewish apostles who worked with Him entirely. According to the Pagans, Jesus and all the others upon whom this character is predicated are personifications of the sun, (even Malachi 4:2 mentions him and calls him the "sun" of righteousness"

Concluding, let's talk about *firsts*, it'll explain the pattern of behavior of these pagan Christs for one. Isaiah 14:14 and wanting to be like the, Most High as the root cause analysis of pagan behavior. The scripture states, Lucifer who is Satan the orchestrator of Paganism and idol worship; the duplicator and perverter of all that is good, the one who appears, masquerades as the angel of light (2 Corinthians 11:14), seeking who he may devour as he roars around (1 Peter 5:8) said, "I will ascend above the heights of the clouds; I will be like the most High."

The examples following are implicating the patterns of cloned idolatry understanding the orchestrator of the cloning. Jesus was, is and is to come; the Alpha and Omega, the first and last (revelation 1:9). Bright and morning Star (Revelation 22:16), the Creator (Genesis 1:1; John 1:1)

Satan, wants to be like the Most High, arch angel now in fallen state (Luke 10:18-20), defied The Creator as a creature and was kicked out with a third of the angels. He is the son of the morning (Isaiah 14:12-23); wanting to cease the day; Creature

Adam, first man from the recreated world whom Satan refuses to serve (first book of Adam and Eve), because according to Lucifer, he was there first.

Lucifer sees woman, takes advantage of their ignorance of who they really are (*first* gods of the earth) (Genesis 3:1), created by the Creator to reflect Him, they looked like God which Lucifer apparently sought to control.

Satan impregnates Eve and her *first born son* isn't Adamic but Satanic (Genesis 3:15), literally. The murderous trait is passed down from father to son (Exodus 34:6-7) and seeks to kill his younger half Adamic brother Abel (Genesis 4). Seth is his replacement.

The first Lamech from Cain, "kills a man to his wounding, a young man to his hurt" and lives to tell about it to his 2 wives Genesis 4:23-24). Amazing the "coincidence" that he was also the father of Tubal-Cain, the fathers of the Masons. Here we see the satanic murderous trait incepted by Cain through Satan play out in their bloodline since blood comes from the father, figuratively speaking it's not known if Satan has blood but Cain did.

The second Lamech (Genesis 5:30-31) is from Seth. He happens to be Enoch, and Methuselah's descendant and Noah's father <u>Genesis 5:29</u> and (Genesis 5:12-25). Reason he comes into the picture, is the very reason we're having this conversation. The "hybriding" of the human race produces giants filled with violence the earth couldn't take more. God through Noah wipes out their giant race and begins the human race a third recorded time with 8 people (Genesis 7:6).

Abraham, and his two sons. The first needs no introduction (Genesis 17:20). Due to the painful existence and background of his story, we're not sure if he held a grudge for being put out of his father's house at 13 but he sure was the first son rejected. He wasn't Gods will bearing the covenant, the second son was (Genesis 21:1-7). This first born's rejection, second son's blessed trend is carried on throughout the next generation.

Isaac, Ishmael's younger brother is the chosen one who gives birth to twins (Genesis 25:19-34)! Esau was red and hairy and Jacob smooth. They are said to have wrestled in the womb whereby Jacob was to come out first but Esau breached his birth, earned his birth right which is later stolen by younger twin Jacob. Jacob becomes the chosen boy even though Esau was groomed to be accepted by his father Isaac. I believe deep down, Isaac tried to break the cycle but mom Rebecca had better plans and assists with the retrieving of the birthright.

Pharaoh the pagan Egyptian and Joseph the chosen savior of Israel's Egypt or Egypt's Israel, and surrounding areas.

Ramses the first heir, Moses the chosen leader, delivering the Israelites from bondage which their forefathers (by God), put them in. Famine caused them to move to Egypt. Isaac however had been cautioned not to go to Israel because Ishmael was part Egyptian and needed to be safe.

All these firsts represented a "movement's" significant rebellion or controversy that opposes/d or attempted to play parts designed for true covenant. The seconds, like the blessings Jacob pronounced on Joseph's sons (Genesis 48:5; 17) putting the second son on the right hand and first son on his left while annunciating the blessings (Genesis 48:20).

I could go on and on regarding this Pagan - Covenant relationship all throughout bible history including Adam being the first fallen "god" or deity having been created in the very image of God and Christ the second Adam born of a woman, ascended to the Right Hand of God as God who couldn't fall.

The mitochondrial DNA of Mary dated back to that of Noah's wife which dated back to Eve and from here cane parallel religions, with the truth swallowing up deceit for the glory of God Himself and extension of His gospel.

The True Messiah rules and reigns and to find truth; one must return to where He was once incepted; to those writings from the First True Apostles who have sent word throughout their lifetime and given True Accounts of His Person, witnessed and recorded. No need to falter. Faith unfeigned moves mountains (James 1:8) and if anyone lacks wisdom, it is readily available when we request it (James 1:5).

9

Son of God vs. Son of Man

Keeping Things in Perspective

Jesus the Corrector of many errors had yet to correct one more err often and easily overlooked. Just like the pagans likened Christ "the Son of God" to the Sun of God even scripture in Malachi 4:2 where the Son became the Sun, reflecting translation at this time to be given to the gentiles the Pagans, He throughout the gospels referred to Himself as the Son of man.

26 (twenty six) times, Jesus the Son of God is recorded although the original meaning needing emphasis to distinguish between the son of God image to the Son of God from **1 Corinthians 15:28**, **Psalm 2:7**, **Hebrews 1:5**, **Matthew 3:17**, **Matthew 17:5**, **Mark 1:11**, **John 1:14**, **1 John 4:10**, **John 14:13**, **John 5:19**, **John 5:26**, **Mark 14:61**, **Mark 5:7**, **Luke 8:28**, **Acts 13:33**, **Hebrews 5:5**, **Mark 9:7**, **Luke 3:22**, **2 Peter 1:17**, **Luke 9:35**, **Romans 1:4**, **Matthew 2:15**, **Luke 20:13**, **Hebrews 1:8**, **1 John 5:9**, and **1 John 5:10**.

16 (sixteen) times Jesus is referred to as the Son of Man. From **Matthew 8:20**, **Matthew 9:6**, **Matthew 11:19**, **Matthew 16:13**, **Matthew 18:11**, **Matthew 24:27**, **Mark 8:38**, **Luke 18:8**, **John 1:51**, **John 5:27**, **John 6:53**, **John 12:23**, **John 13:31**. **Acts 7:56**, to **Revelation 1:13** with Jesus Himself and John the revelator/disciple referring to Him as the Son of Man in correction to the myth and ideology that He could be equal to His own

created beings i.e. the Sons of God aka angels. There are even times when scripture referred to Him as Angel with a capital "A" describing His pre-eminence and statute and ranking among the angels but never equated to angels. Again I would like to refer to Isaiah 14:14 where Satan ascended to the heights of the clouds to be like the Most High led to his demise. Christ would never be on the same level as Satan! This very broad emphasis to His pre-eminence needs to be re-emphasized to separate Him from his created (spirit) beings as they are charged with folly (Job 4:18), yet Christ is Holy; especially when relating to soul winning and teachings. It can be misleading.

The Greek for "firstborn" is proto with tikto which would give us "firstborn" and that is what we find here in <u>Colossians 1:15</u>. The Greek for "first created" would be proto with ktizo, and it is not used here.

The Biblical use of the word "firstborn" is most interesting. It can mean the first born child in a family (<u>Luke 2:7</u>), but it can also mean **"<u>pre-eminence.</u>"** In <u>Psalm 89:20</u>, <u>27</u> we find that the LORD says, "I have found David My servant; with My holy oil I have anointed him . . . And I will make him the firstborn, the highest of the kings of the earth" (ESV). As we can see, David, who was the last-one born in his family, was called the firstborn by God. ***This is a title of preeminence.***

Firstborn does not require a meaning of first created. "Firstborn" can mean the first born person in a family, and it can also be a title of preeminence which is transferable.

See Genesis 41:51–52 where we find Joseph calling his first-born son Manasseh and the second son he named Ephraim. However, in Jeremiah 31:9, the LORD says, "…For I am a Father to Israel, and Ephraim *is* My firstborn."

Jesus is God in flesh (<u>John 1:1</u>, <u>14</u>) and is also the first born son of Mary. In addition, He is the pre-eminent one in all things.

Jesus is called the first-born, not the first-created. The word "first-born" (Greek word "prototokos") signifies priority. In the culture of the Ancient Near East, the first-born was not necessarily the oldest child. First-born referred not to birth order but to rank. The first-born possessed the inheritance and leadership.

<u>Six times</u> the Lord Jesus is declared to be the first-born of God (see Romans 8:29; Colossians 1:15, 18; Hebrews 1:6; 12:23; Revelation 1:5). These passages declare the preexistence, the sovereignty, and the redemption that Christ offers. Thus, the phrase "first-born of all creation" proclaims Christ's preeminence. He created the universe. He is the Ruler of creation!

Referring to Christ as the Son of man takes us back to the story of creation where God (the Father-will, Son-body and Holy Spirit-spirit) decided among themselves to create man in their very own image meaning this man would possess all three attributes (father, son and Holy spirit) within him as His makers possessed; and they did. This passage of scripture may explain in layman terms and sum it up. "And so it is written, the first man Adam was made a living soul; the last Adam *was made* a quickening spirit. Howbeit that *was* not first which is spiritual, but that which is natural; and afterward that which is spiritual. The first man was of the dust of the earth, the second man from heaven. As was the earthly man, so also are those who are of the earth; and as is the heavenly man, so also are those who are of heaven. And just as we have borne the likeness of the earthly man, so also shall we bear the likeness of the heavenly man" 1 Corinthians 15:45-49.

Christ and Adam are almost always seen as one and the same thing; the only difference is their pre-eminence and destiny. Due to the folly of man, Christ came to redeem him. He, though man, was given all the qualities of His creator, only subject to Him it was not revealed to him that he was a real god subject to God alone and Satan hated it. Angel spirits were never made man; Adam was which brought dissention as Satan sought to overthrow him (Him) and his (His) dominion as he did. Adam was a mirror of Christ who ruled overall and point of contention which led to their ousting from the garden of Eden through adulterating that which was Holy and bearing that which was evil – hence the term eve-ill. Eve became ill through the seed that germinated in her body and the garden could not receive the seed of Satan. It was Holy.

Upon studying symbolisms in scripture, it came to my understanding that God "metaphorically" likened people to trees. Since we're both planted on or in soil and have potential of bearing fruit. There are several references in scripture reflecting this theory like Psalms 1:3 and Jeremiah 17:8 where references to people who live accordingly will be like trees planted by the rivers of waters who's fruitfulness will not cease because of the cycle of unending watering due to strategic location by its life source; water. Jesus in Mark 8:24 asked the blind man he just healed what He saw. My guess is as good as yours. He already knew but wanted the man to be specific and said "he saw men like trees walking" and couldn't quite clearly identify men from trees.

This brings me to the next finding. The two trees in the garden forbidden to Adam and Eve were representing two people they were to avoid. The one is obvious because he possessed knowledge of good and evil and was likened to the tree of knowledge of good and evil unless enchanted these trees were given human personifications and characteristics because Jesus wasn't referring to trees at all. He was referring to beings. One was Satan/Lucifer himself. He had the knowledge of good and evil. He had been in the presence of God Almighty and was exposed to His Good and exposed himself to the badness and evil that comes with defiance and conflict. He was acquainted, accustomed and exposed to both good and evil. The next tree/person was life giving which symbolized either Christ or the Holy Spirit. Having researched the scriptures and how God treats the Holy Spirit whose breath was breathed in Adam, warnings were given not to blaspheme Him because the sin of blasphemy against the Holy Spirit isn't forgiven nor will it ever in Matthew 12:30-32. Those two "trees" were not available to them and they were to steer clear.

(Genesis 3:15 "And I will put enmity between you and the woman, and **between your seed** ("Cainites") and **_her Seed_** (Christ); He shall bruise your head {crushing it completely}, and you shall bruise **_His heel_** {persecution, crucifixion, death, and resurrection})." Christ called Himself the Son of Man having descended from His own likeness Adam as He stated and not the Son of God as he was referred. He corrected theology without anyone taking note of His Personage as Son of Man. As Adam was 100% flesh and 100% spirit so was Christ 100% flesh and 100% Spirit. Only and like Lucifer, Adam fell but Christ who didn't/couldn't fall was resurrected. The earth couldn't keep Him. There was no sin found in Him.

Christ, the Rock that no one handles, "cut out without hands," the King from the beginning, whom no one created, Creator of the Universe, will crush these kingdoms and establishments of the earth and establish His Own as He willed from the beginning as we understand it. This Kingdom of God will last forever and it will be a Kingdom of Peace and He will rule and no one will take it away from Him as Adam lost his. He is the second Adam who defeated and overcome the devil. The era will be ushered in with the binding of Satan for 1000 years (revelation 20); a time to look forward to.

It was pleasure writing this book as I look forward to what's ahead. I look forward to the revealing of Christ, His Glorious appearing and I thank you for taking the time to partake of this communing together in spirit. May the words of this book enrich, empower and enlighten you to seek out the Utmost Higher Infallible Unchanging Truth.

References were taken from:

The World Book Encyclopedia; *Library of the World's Myths and Legends (Persian Mythology)*; *Stories of the Bible on TV* – *Historians*; J. M. Robertson, T. W. Doane, F. Cument, J. G. Frazer; *The Origins of the Mithraic Mysteries* by David Ulansey

Other References:

Wikipedia,
https://www.chabad.org/library/article_cdo/aid/112333/jewish/Nimrod-and-Abraham.htm
https://divineheartofgod.org/2013/09/09/the-first-words-adam-said-to-god-the-father/
https://en.wikipedia.org/wiki/Napoleon_and_the_Catholic_Church
https://www.churchofjesuschrist.org/study/manual/doctrines-of-the-gospel-student-manual/27-sabbath?lang=eng
https://en.wikipedia.org/wiki/Nicene_Christianity
https://en.wikipedia.org/wiki/Early_Muslim_conquests
https://www.history.com/topics/ancient-rome/goths-and-visigoths
https://forum.christogenea.org/viewtopic.php?f=3&t=1770
https://www.historyfiles.co.uk/KingListsEurope/BarbarianHeruli.htm
https://courses.lumenlearning.com/boundless-worldhistory/chapter/byzantium-the-new-rome/
http://science.howstuffworks.com/life/evolution/female-ancestor.htm
biblebb.com/files/KSS/kss-rahab.htm
reikirays.com
http://www.wwco.com/religion/believe/believe_34.html
(http://science.howstuffworks.com/life/evolution/female-ancestor.htm)
http://www.mhrc.net/mitochondrialEve.htm
A course in miracles
https://jdstone.org/cr/files/mithraschristianity.html
http://www4.westminster.edu/staff/brennie/rel101/daniel.htm
https://medium.com/@thomas.dohling/the-greek-for-firstborn-is-proto-with-tikto-which-would-give-us-firstborn-and-that-is-what-we-f00e68db381f
https://ehp.niehs.nih.gov/doi/10.1289/EHP2268